Water Babies

Water Babies

THE HIDDEN LIVES OF BABY WETLAND BIRDS

William Burt

The Countryman Press
A division of W. W. Norton & Company
Independent Publishers Since 1923

Frontispiece:
PIPING PLOVER (YOUNG) – OLD LYME,
CONNECTICUT, MAY 2013

The Countryman Press
www.countrymanpress.com

A division of
W. W. Norton & Company, Inc.
500 Fifth Avenue, New York, N.Y. 10110
www.wwnorton.com

For information about special discounts
for bulk purchases, please contact
W. W. Norton Special Sales at
specialsales@wwnorton.com
or 800-233-4830

Printed in China

Water Babies
978-1-58157-305-3

1 2 3 4 5 6 7 8 9 0

BLACK TERNS (YOUNG) – TOWNER
COUNTY, NORTH DAKOTA, JUNE 2011

TO THE MEMORY OF ROGER TORY PETERSON

CONTENTS

SNOWY EGRETS (JUVENILE) – JOHNS COUNTY, FLORIDA, JUNE 2011

WHIMBREL (YOUNG) – CHURCHILL, MANITOBA, JULY 2011

INTRODUCTION

First, it was the rails. It took me 14 years to photograph those skulkers of the marsh, and I was sorry to be done with them.

My fascination had been sparked one June day years ago, when I was still a teenager. I'd walked up to the edge of a small pond that morning when a strange unbirdlike bird stepped out before me and plunged in, dog-paddled straight across, and slipped into the weeds and grasses on the other side. I ran around at once and thrashed through every last square foot of vegetation, several times, but it was no use: the bird had disappeared. It was a rail—a Clapper Rail, as I later learned, from the very man who wrote my *Field Guide*—and it had left its mark. Even today, some fifty years after that June morning by the pond, I'm especially drawn to birds few people ever see.

After the rails, it was the bug-eyed bitterns. I chased after them for several summers, in North Dakota and Connecticut and a few marshes in between. Then I set my sights on the nocturnal ghost birds of the uplands, the nightjars. They kept me looping about the map for the next half a dozen years, between New England and the Carolinas, from Texas to Saskatchewan.

Rails, bitterns, nightjars—and what now? The end was near, I knew, or thought I knew, but I kept busy with some sneaky songbirds such as Henslow's Sparrow and Connecticut Warbler. And then, just when it seemed imagination had abandoned me entirely and I would run out my string, it dawned on me. For two or three weeks every year, the wetlands teemed with these new downy beings most of which I'd never seen, or even known about: the *Water Babies*.

Here was a whole new catalogue of creatures, and challenges enough to last a lifetime.

9

SEMIPALMATED PLOVER (YOUNG) – CHURCHILL, MANITOBA, JULY 2011

The "Babies"

The "babies" are the downy young of ducks, grebes, gallinules, shorebirds, herons, and other birds of shores and wetlands—those that "get their feet wet," as it were; and it's little wonder that so few of us have ever seen them. They are not only small, but quick, adept at hiding, and superbly camouflaged.

But above all else, they are endearing. From the comic-monster herons to the fuzzy ducklings and stick-legged sandpipers, these tots have personality—and *spunk*. They cannot know it, happily, but the chances are as good as not that in their first two weeks they will be snatched away and fed in pieces to some other mother's young; yet from the moment they can stand and walk or swim they know exactly what they are supposed to do, and they get on with it. They buzz or bob along with all the purpose in the world, as if there was a life to live. A future.

Looking back at all these water-loving birds I've photographed, I'm struck by the *variety* of wetlands they inhabit. From the scruffy pool-strewn arctic tundra to the lush green sloughs and potholes of Saskatchewan and North Dakota, and from the open shores, sturdy cattail marshes, and soft *Spartina* meadows of the mid-Atlantic seaboard to the jungly swamps, lagoons, and mangrove keys of Florida, Louisiana, and the Gulf . . . the range is nearly endless.

The birds themselves, as well: what a fantastical array they are, adults and young alike. Web-footed ducks and lobe-toed coots, and grebes, and phalaropes; stilt-legged herons, storks, and ibises, and shorebirds with bills long and short, bills recurved and decurved and straight as a railroad spike; the gulls that sail and terns that plunge-dive, rainbow-colored gallinules that strut on lily pads, and bitterns that stretch upright like the reeds: they vary so much in their equipment and how they use it that you might suppose their paths would never cross. But in the wetlands they all come together, live, and raise their young, all drawn by the one essential need: water.

Without the water—and the wetlands—these birds wouldn't be.

RUDDY DUCK (ADULT HEN AND YOUNG) – TOWNER COUNTY, NORTH DAKOTA, AUGUST 2010

The Species and the Families

The *species* to follow represent 10 *families* of birds—the grebes (*Podicipedidae*), the herons and bitterns (*Ardeidae*), the waterfowl (*Anatidae*), and so forth—but they are grouped here into seven chapters, with a little juggling for thematic purposes. The bitterns, for example, so unlike the other, showier of herons (*Ardeidae*), are presented in a separate chapter of their own, while the three families of shorebirds (plovers, sandpipers, and stilts and avocets) are combined as one. The species appear not always in their proper phylogenetic order, but in a sequence that makes for the most effective presentation of the photographs.

The photos are devoted mostly to the downy young birds, but each "baby" is accompanied by at least one view of the adult it will become.

What *Kind* of Baby—*Altricial,* or *Precocial*?

Not all bird babies are endearing—least of all the *altricial* babies.

The young of robins, bluebirds, finches, and other backyard songbirds are *altricial*: that is to say, they are hatched naked, sightless, and unable to feed themselves, or even leave the nest. A newly hatched altricial bird is a meaty, embryonic-looking thing with a big mouth, big eyes like blueberries, and a big head that wobbles.

The chicks of shorebirds, ducks, grebes, and most other swimmers, on the other hand—which is to say most of the *Water Babies*—are *precocial*. They are so well developed in the egg already that within mere hours of hatching they scoot off the nest to seek their fortunes, never to return.

Some young birds don't fit into either category. The herons, egrets, and other wading birds in Chapter II, for instance, hatch open-eyed and fuzzed with down, like precocial birds; but like altricial chicks, they cannot feed themselves, or leave the nest site. These birds are called *semi-altricial*.

The gulls and terns of Chapter V, conversely, are *semi-precocial*. They too hatch open-eyed and downy, but they cannot feed themselves; yet if danger threatens they can shuffle off and hide, or even swim away.

CATTLE EGRETS (YOUNG) – MILLERS LAKE,
LOUISIANA, JUNE 2010

EARED GREBES (ADULT AND YOUNG) – CRANE LAKE SASKATCHEWAN, JULY 1995

I

The Ferry-boating Grebes

THESE FUNKY-LOOKING WATER BIRDS RESEMBLE DUCKS, BUT THEY ARE SLIGHTER, WITH SLIM BILLS AND LONG, SLIM NECKS LIKE PERISCOPES. Like loons, grebes are terrific divers, able to propel themselves great distances beneath the water, and to stay submerged for minutes at a time. *Minutes*, literally: the Horned Grebe has been recorded as staying under for a full three minutes and swimming some 500 feet before resurfacing.

500 feet: that's nearly the length of two football playing fields.

From their first helpless days in ovo to their last—except for the two times each year when they migrate from one water body to another—these birds spend their every living moment on, or in, the water. Even loons will sometimes haul out onto solid land, if only in concession to their nesting duties, but not grebes; even their nests sit on the water.

They are odd birds in other ways, too: in their propensity for eating feathers, for instance, and in their slow submarine-like way of sinking. But niftiest of all is what the young birds do for transportation. No sooner are the chicks free of the eggshell than they tumble off the nest into the water, swim to their nearest parent, and climb up onto its back. And there they sit, like sightseers on a ferry, while the parent does the driving.

But they are not riding for the fun of it as much as for the warmth. If left to bob and swim for themselves in those first days, they would soon chill and die.

Above and right:
(ADULTS AND YOUNG) – STUTSMAN COUNTY, NORTH DAKOTA, JUNE 2013
Just moments after hatching, the chicks climb onto their parent's back, where they will be transported for the next four weeks.
The youngsters can sit up and watch, participate, enjoy the ride, or put down their heads and rest; or they can tuck in underneath a wing and sleep, immune to the big busy world about them. And if danger threatens, the whole boatload will go under in an instant. All parties hold their breath, the chicks clamp on to their parent's feathers with their bills, and down they go.
And when the boat resurfaces, the party motors off again: heads up and eyes trained straight ahead, as if it never happened.

WESTERN GREBE
Aechmophorus occidentalis

The "swan grebe," it once was called, and like a swan it is: a long-necked bird of picture-perfect grace and poise. On calm, smooth-water days it glides across its western lake with neck and head held high, like a distinguished lady. A Lady of the Lake.

But it appears in other roles, as well. When a Western Grebe glides closer and you see what a poor little fish might see—the cold red eyes, the long slim speartip of a bill—it is no longer quite so ladylike. It's menacing. And if you glimpse it in the waters of a stormy day, emerging for a moment in the lashing surf, then disappearing, you might think you've seen some creature of the ancient deep: a plesiosaur?

The stub-billed youngster, on the other hand, is about as without menace as a living thing can be. Unlike the striped young of the smaller grebes, the downy Western is dove-gray above and lighter gray below, with no marks other than a small, straw-yellow skin patch on the crown, which flushes red with hunger or excitement.

It has no other color, no stripes on the head, no spots or patterns anywhere: no razzmatazz at all, only gray. Yet it's the loveliest of grebe chicks. Only the lighter-colored young of its close relative, the Clark's Grebe, can compare, and that one's really just a paler, poorer copy.

Above:
WESTERN GREBES (ADULT AND YOUNG) – CRANE LAKE, SASKATCHEWAN, JULY 1995
The ornithologist Frank Chapman wrote that a young Western Grebe chick "will crawl into one's hand rather than remain in the water."

Left:
WESTERN GREBES (ADULT AND YOUNG) – STUTSMAN COUNTY, NORTH DAKOTA, JUNE 2013

EARED GREBE
Podiceps nigricollis

No other grebe, indeed no other bird, is as out-and-out aquatic as this red-eyed diver of the West. It is a grebe in the extreme, and not only has it little need to fly, except on migration, but for up to ten months of the year it actually can't. Aside from breeding and molting, the Eared Grebe has little else to do throughout its long months on the lakes and ponds but eat and pack on fat, in preparation for migration.

No other bird, except for those odd few that cannot fly at all, is flightless for so long a period.

The Eared is the most abundant of the grebes, and one of the most gregarious. Where conditions suit it, in the reed-littered bays and coves of western lakes, it nests in floating cities of a thousand pairs or more. The nests themselves are soggy, slovenly affairs, and often packed so close together that the old-time bird man Herbert K. Job described their congregations as "the slums of bird-dom."

So closely packed was one grebe "slum" in North Dakota, back in 1883, that 25 nests were counted in a space approximately 10 by 20 feet: about the size of a home kitchen.

Above and left:
(ADULT AND YOUNG) – SIDEWOOD, SASKATCHEWAN, JULY 2012
Could a young bird and its parent possibly look more different?
If the two were not together, you might never guess that they
belong to the same bird family, let alone the same species.

Above and right:
EARED GREBES (ADULT AND YOUNG) – SIDEWOOD, SASKATCHEWAN, JULY 2012
When a parent wants to free itself of chicks, it simply rises, flaps its wings, and shakes them off.

23

They *EAT* Feathers?

All grebes do. They eat their own, and others', and lots of them. Great wads of feathers have been found in their dissected stomachs, even the stomachs of the downy young. The ornithologist Frank Chapman once counted 331 in the stomach of a Western Grebe "not more than three days old."

Newly hatched grebe chicks have been known to swallow feathers before ingesting any actual food. What for? Presumably, the feathers help protect the bird's digestive tract from the hard, sharp bones of the fish they eat: either physically, as a barrier, or physiologically, by slowing down digestion so that bones have time to soften or dissolve. Indeed, the more important fish is to a given species' diet, the more feathers it will eat.

Might these strange birds evolve in other ways, even more bizarre? Eliot Porter, the photographer, believed they could. "Is it not reasonable," he mused, "that certain families of birds, such as grebes and penguins, may become viviparous, incubating their eggs internally and thus become an entirely aquatic mode of life? To me birds seem capable of almost any adaptation."

Try It Sometime

Wade out into a prairie lake in even the most artfully concealing photo blind, however cautiously, and you'll watch in dismay as the birds swim out ahead beyond your reach, or peel away to the side. The ducks and coots, the Pied-billed Grebes and Franklin's Gulls—they don't quite trust this new craft on their waters and they keep their distance. All birds but one, that is: the little grebe with the red eyes and golden ear tufts.

Whether diving, bobbing up with food in beak, or ferry-boating chicks on its back, or even drifting with its head down, fast asleep, it makes no difference: the Eared Grebe will carry on as if you were not even there.

EARED GEBES (ADULT AND YOUNG) – SIDEWOOD, SASKATCHEWAN, JULY 2012
Within an hour of hatching, the chicks can climb, swim, and beg for food.
Eared Grebe chicks are "back-brooded" for about ten days, at which point their parents separate and each takes custody of half of the remaining brood—though the remaining brood by this time, after losses to predation, may leave them only one chick each: if that.

PIED-BILLED GREBE
Podilymbus podiceps

The plumage of this plain brown diver looks more like a scrap of old discarded carpet, or the pelage of a rodent. It is a ratty-looking bird.

The Pied-billed Grebe is *the* familiar grebe in much of North America, and in the East it is essentially the only nesting grebe. But it's also the wariest, by far. If it feels threatened in the least, or even noticed, it casts a wary eye on the intruder and steams away, or dives, or simply sinks: it expels air from its body, compresses feathers, and goes down like a submarine.

And once it's down, it is as good as down for good. You can mark the spot and wait all afternoon for it to re-emerge, and when it doesn't you might think it's either drowned or been taken by some underwater monster. Of course it has come up: a few hundred feet away, perhaps, or in a stand of reeds where you can't see it; but it has come up.

Drab though it is, the Pied-billed's chicks are jazzy little jobs with black-and-white striped heads and necks and small pink patches on their faces. Chicks of all the small grebe species have this snake-like striping, and are so alike that unless you see them plainly with their parents you might never know which belong to which.

So much do adult and young birds differ that you might think you are seeing creatures of entirely different species.

Above:
(ADULT) – ST. JOHNS COUNTY, FLORIDA, MARCH 2011
Hell Diver, Water Witch: what better nicknames? More than one of the old-time bird men tried to shoot one of these canny divers, only to find that each time they pulled the trigger it had already dived, and their shot struck only water.

Right:
(YOUNG) – CRANE LAKE, SASKATCHEWAN, JULY 2000

PIED-BILLED GREBES (ADULT AND YOUNG) –
CRANE LAKE, SASKATCHEWAN, JULY 2000
*The homely Pied-billed is the least inclined
of the grebes to carry young on its back, and
does so only when the chicks are less than one
week old.*

RED-NECKED GREBE
Podiceps grisegena

Unlike the other prairie-nesting grebes, which tend to mass together in vast floating colonies, the Red-necked is inclined to solitude, more in the manner of the Horned and Pied-billed Grebes, though it does sometimes occur in scattered colonies of up to a dozen pairs or more. While it nests sparingly on prairie lakes with Eared and Western Grebes, its major haunts are the pond-dotted wooded regions north of the Great Plains, in the Canadian West.

The Red-necked Grebe has long been considered one of the wariest of water birds, perhaps because it tends to be so solitary, but some individuals are anything but shy. The bird in the photograph, for instance, seen here basking in the late-day sunlight of Saskatchewan without a worry in the world: it showed not the slightest apprehension of the floating blind just 40 feet away and closing in.

Even at the sl-*ap* of the camera shutter, it refused to raise an eye. And then, as I framed up to fire a second time, surprise: out from beneath its folded wings popped a striped head.

It was a downy chick, and it had been there all the time, tucked in and sleeping.

(ADULT AND YOUNG) – CRANE LAKE, SASKATCHEWAN, JULY 2000
There is no mistaking this stripe-headed grebe chick. The black bars on its face are neater, cleaner, and more handsomely pronounced than any other. And it is the only chick whose bill is yellow.

BLACK-CROWNED NIGHT-HERONS (YOUNG) – MCLEAN COUNTY, NORTH DAKOTA, JULY 2013
Lunging, snapping, and brandishing their wings like lobster claws: a madhouse of young herons.

II

The Comic Monsters: Long-legged Waders

YOU SEE THEM ALMOST ANYWHERE IN THE DEEP SOUTH, POISED GRACEFULLY IN YARDS AND ALONG HIGHWAY STRIPS OR LOITERING WITHOUT PERMISSION ON GOLF COURSES AND THE GROUNDS OF GATED COMPOUNDS, LIKE LAWN ORNAMENTS RUN WILD. They stand idle on the banks of ditches and on fishing piers, boat launches, and the dikes of water treatment plants, and stalk the waters of congenial nature centers, wildlife management areas, and wildlife refuges. They are no more exotic to most people than their fellow shoppers in a mall.

But to see them in their own stick-nested cities, and for a gallery of nestling faces you will not forget, you need to venture into haunts a little less convenient: swamps.

For their first week or two, the young birds are half-naked, pathetic-looking things with beaks too big and heads that sag, as if hatched too soon. And then, when they have sprouted pinfeathers and a few springy "hairs" on top, they appear to be compounded of odd parts, like frizzy Frankensteins. At two to four weeks old, your average heron is part goof, part mad professor, and part scarecrow-monster of your worst bad dreams.

But they're not really all that scary. They may raise their wings and hiss and take a few mock jabs at you, but in the end they're funny-paper monsters only, and they'll only make you laugh.

(YOUNG) – ST. JOHNS COUNTY, FLORIDA, JUNE 2011

Unlike young ducks and grebes and sandpipers, the young of herons are bound to their nests for weeks, and they continue to be fed by their indulgent parents for weeks after that. Their food is mostly fish, stored in the parents' gullets and produced on demand as a regurgitated bouillabaisse.

SNOWY EGRET
Egretta thula

An easy, walk-through tour of a wild heron rookery? There is such a thing, in Florida, at either of two tourist meccas known as "alligator farms." These bustling sites leave much to be desired aesthetically, perhaps, for they are often peopled by the busload, but they do allow you views of long-legged wading birds at home within their nesting colonies, which you would have a hard time getting elsewhere: Tricolored Herons mostly, but also Wood Storks, and the three common egrets: Cattle, Great, and Snowy.

The Snowy has the fanciest of courtship plumes, for which it was once slaughtered nearly to extinction—so that fancy ladies could wear feathers in their hats. By 1910, after decades of shooting, the Snowy population was so devastated that extinction was believed inevitable. But by that time, thanks to an enlightened public and the passage of new legislation, the killing was at last well on its way to a forced halt. By the onset of the First World War, the plumes of herons were once again, as they say, worn only by their rightful owners.

But *alligator farms*? Why would the birds debase themselves?

When establishing a rookery, the long-legged wading birds require a stand of trees or shrubs, standing water, and one other thing: security. To secure their homes from predators, they need an armed police force, as it were; and what better than an on-site, round-the-clock on-duty force of alligators? If the standing water and the elevation of the nests do not discourage prowling foxes or raccoons, the gators will.

It's a symbiotic bargain, good for the herons and the gators both. The odd fallen nestling is snapped up at once, of course, and that's what's in it for the gators—the odd windfall picnic now and then—but it's a small price for the birds to pay for 24-hour protection against total loss. A single night raid by a few raccoons or foxes could clean out an entire colony.

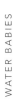

Above:
SNOWY EGRET (ADULT AND YOUNG) – ST. JOHNS COUNTY, FLORIDA, JUNE 2011

Right:
SNOWY EGRET (YOUNG) – ST. JOHNS COUNTY, FLORIDA, JUNE 2011

GREAT EGRET
Ardea alba

O f the various egret rookeries that Roger Tory Peterson saw over his long life, and they were many, one held for him a beauty beyond all others: Cranetown, as it was called, in a tall stand of cypresses at Reelfoot Lake, Tennessee. "It has that Chinese print quality," he wrote, "with which I had vested my early preconceived visions of what an egret colony must look like: graceful alabaster birds in a wonderland of tall cypress."

It is unlikely that his white bird wonderland still thrives today. In the 1950s, the story goes, a Hollywood film director ordered that a charge of dynamite be set off in the swamp so that the birds might rise and fly and prettify a sequence for his movie, *Raintree County*. The birds did rise and fly, just as directed; and they kept on flying, never to return.

So we make do with other, lesser white bird wonderlands today: at the Audubon Plantation and Gardens near Charleston, South Carolina, for example, where a small Great Egret rookery convenes each year in a red maple swamp.

Above:
(ADULT) – CHARLESTON, SOUTH CAROLINA, APRIL 2009

Left:
(YOUNG) – KISSIMMEE, FLORIDA, MAY 2012
Speechless, with heads up and bug-eyed on their stems, three siblings look on in amazement as a Cattle Egret (outside picture) yanks a stick out from their nest.

THE COMIC MONSTERS: LONG-LEGGED WADERS

Above and right:
GRTEAT EGRET (ADULT) – CHARLESTON, SOUTH CAROLINA, APRIL 2009
*In breeding season, the adults display the ornate "aigrettes" once so
coveted by milliners—and the vain ladies who would wear them.*

THE COMIC MONSTERS: LONG-LEGGED WADERS

REDDISH EGRET
Egretta rufescens

Most heron species stand and wait for prey to come their way, like living statuary, but not this one; its mode of feeding is what the biologists would call "Disturb and Chase." It leaps and prances through lagoons and tidal pools, stirring up small fish and other manageable prey—and seizing it.

An active, *energetic* heron? In this case, that's not an oxymoron.

Even young birds practice the Disturb and Chase, from the day their feet first meet the mud and sand, though all they're really chasing is each other. When they leave the nest, six weeks or more remain before they can catch their own live prey, but in the meantime they skip over sandbars and through shallows, in pursuit of parent birds with food but also their own siblings, in an everlasting contest for first place in line.

These sandbar hooligans are born to chivy one another, and they do it constantly: for practice, and for play, and for each other's food.

Above:
(JUVENILE) – TAMPA BAY, FLORIDA, JUNE 2010

Right:
(YOUNG) – TAMPA BAY, FLORIDA, JUNE 2010
Free of the nest at last, a young bird splashes through the shallows in a practice run for the day when it will catch its own prey.

43

Above:
REDDISH EGRET (JUVENILE) – TAMPA BAY, FLORIDA, JUNE 2010

Right:
REDDISH EGRET (ADULT) – TAMPA BAY, FLORIDA, JUNE 2010
Unlike the two white egrets, Great and Snowy, the Reddish has never fully recovered from the depredations of late-nineteenth-century plume hunters. It is today the rarest of the North American herons, with the exception of the so-called "Great White," a color morph of the Great Blue confined to the Florida Keys.

THE COMIC MONSTERS: LONG-LEGGED WADERS

CATTLE EGRET
Bubulcus ibis

Want to see a southern countryside turned white by egrets, and packed full of egret nests? The time is early June and the place Millers Lake, Louisiana, in the cattle-ranching lowlands north of Lafayette. Be there at dawn and you'll see Cattle Egrets by the hundreds, streaming out from their night roosts across the pastures, and staged in the treetops like a fairyland of blooms.

Get in a boat, motor up into the swampy mazes among rows of buttonbush and elderberry, and you'll see their nests, about head-high, slapped into any fork or crotch that will accept them. They are crude, ad hoc affairs of sticks, unlined, and bristling with sharp snags you'd think might interfere with feeding—not to say endanger the eyes of the young for whom the nests were fashioned in the first place.

The nests are endless, each one as shabby as the next, and you'd think the parents would do better; but the chicks don't seem to care. The drowsy youngest couldn't care for anything but sleep and food, and the alert ones have more pressing things to think about than the crude slum of shrubs and sticks they were born into: like the loss of a parent, say, or hunger, or the big black eyes down in the water watching, just in case.

Above and left:
(YOUNG) – MILLERS LAKE, LOUISIANA, JUNE 2010
In two to three weeks, this forlorn-looking nestling will become a "brancher": a young bird that has left the nest but lingers on a nearby branch to beg for food .

A Story of Invasion

In 1940, no Cattle Egret had ever been seen in North America. Today, it breeds abundantly throughout the South, and it has become an established nesting bird in nearly every state, and even southern Canada. The story of this Afro-Asian native on our continent is one of overseas invasion, conquest, and extended empire—somewhat like that of the British under Queen Victoria.

Its first known occurrence in the Western Hemisphere was in northeastern South America, on the border of Guyana and Suriname, in 1877. Sixty-four years later, in 1941, the first birds were seen in Florida, where they were assumed to be escapees.

Then things began to happen rapidly. In 1951 the species was reported in New Jersey; and on April 23, 1952, a single Cattle Egret was discovered and collected in Wayland, Massachusetts, establishing the first North American specimen record. The very next year, in the spring of 1953, it was proved to nest in Florida; and by 1962, only nine years later, it had bred in Ontario, for the first time in Canada. Over the next half-century, it became established as one of America's most numerous herons.

Today the Cattle Egret is often seen from ships at sea, so there can be no doubt: the bird is searching for new lands to conquer, still.

CATTLE EGRET (ADULT) – KISSIMMEE, FLORIDA, JUNE 2010

Above:
CATTLE EGRET (ADULT) – KISSIMMEE, FLORIDA, APRIL 2014

Left:
CATTLE EGRET (YOUNG) – MILLERS LAKE, LOUISIANA, JUNE 2010

Above:
(YOUNG) – ST. JOHNS COUNTY, FLORIDA, JUNE 2010

Right:
(ADULT) – PALM. BEACH COUNTY, FLORIDA, APRIL 2009

TRICOLORED HERON
Egretta tricolor

Again, one of the best ways to see young herons—at least one of the easiest—is to stop in at the "Alligator Farm" in St. Augustine, Florida.

You line up at the window, pay your $18, and proceed along the boardwalk past the gift shop, past the caged albino gator and the drink stands, the interpretive displays, and out at last over the open waters of a swamp: a puny swamp but real, with real growling gators, and the smell of them. There's a strong smell of fish, too, but that's from the sporadic rain of bird poop, for you're also in the heart of a real living rookery: of herons, egrets, and a few pairs of giant Wood Storks.

Along the boardwalk you can see the same birds' young, both in the nest and out, some by themselves and some in still-life groups of up to four. They sit in place like stuffed birds on exhibit, but with eyes that move; and at the first sign of a parent bird with food, the rest of them moves too.

You'll see young Snowy, Great, and Cattle Egrets, Wood Storks, and Tricolored Herons; and you'll know the Tricolored at once, for it's unlike the young of any other heron. The bill is a long tapered spike, and the neck is long and slim, maroon, with a white stripe running down the center like a snake's. But the best mark is the tawny plumes that spring forth from its head, like the wild hairs of a crazed professor.

The herons of the "gator farm" are all wild birds, all present of their own volition, and all fair game for the camera; yet you can't help feeling that they are

a bit too easy: fish in a barrel, as the saying goes. I left with lots of pictures but
with an uneasy feeling in the gut, as well, as if I had sold out a little.

Just a little.

TRICOLORED HERON (JUVENILE) – ST. JOHNS COUNTY, FLORIDA, JUNE 2010
No other young heron has the tawny mad-professor "hairs" on top.

TRICOLORED HERON (YOUNG) – ST. JOHNS COUNTY, FLORIDA, MAY 2012

Above:
TRICOLORED HERON (YOUNG) – ST. JOHNS COUNTY, FLORIDA, MAY 2010

Right:
TRICOLORED HERON (JUVENILE) – ST. JOHNS COUNTY, FLORIDA, JUNE 2010

BLACK-CROWNED NIGHT-HERON
Nycticorax nycticorax

What a lake, and what an island: what a sordid paradise. It was exactly what I had been looking for, and I had Jackie Jacobson to thank for it.

Like anyone tuned in to birds, I'd often heard its husky *vok* in the late evening sky, and I'd often seen the hulking bird itself, leaned over at the water's edge, as patient as a statue. But I had never seen a nest, or nestlings, and it seemed nobody else had either.

What would a young night-heron look like? It would be some kind of comic monster, surely, like all heron youngsters; but who knows? With that big head and bill it might be something altogether different; and in any case, I couldn't wait to see. But I'd been waiting now for years. Would I live long enough? And if I did, would I still have the strength to haul a camera?

I had begun to have my doubts, when out of nowhere, like a genie to the rescue, had come Jackie.

I was in Jackie's debt already for the day she'd spent helping me in the field a year ago, at Audubon National Wildlife Refuge in North Dakota. She'd helped me find and photograph two downy phalaropes at their big moment of adventure—leaving the nest—and she had almost given me a chance at night-herons, too. Some years earlier, she'd happened across a small group nesting on a cattail island in the middle of a lake, and we paddled out in a canoe to see—but they were gone.

Above:
(YOUNG) – MCLEAN COUNTY, NORTH DAKOTA, JULY 2013
Lunging, snapping, and brandishing their wings like lobster claws: a madhouse of young herons.

Left:
(ADULT) – EVERGLADES N. P., FLORIDA, APRIL, 2009
True, the Black-crowned Night-Heron is seldom seen to swim, but this eager opportunist saw a fish just out of reach—and jumped in after it.

BLACK-CROWNED NIGHT-HERONS (YOUNG) –
MCLEAN COUNTY, NORTH DAKOTA, JULY 2013

Would she keep an ear out for me next year? Maybe ask around among her colleagues, in case anyone should see signs of night-herons nesting? It was a long shot, but I had to ask.

Next year came, and June came too—peak time for nesting—and June went, without a word from North Dakota. It had been a long shot, as I say, and I paid little notice. Another year, perhaps: I'd ask again. But then, to my astonishment—it was the middle of July—Jackie called. "Remember those night-herons you asked about?"

She had indeed inquired among her colleagues, and one had seen herons flying to and from an island in a newly flooded slough, she said—the slough was now effectively a lake—and bless her, she had paddled out in a canoe to find the island swarmed with nesting Ring-billed Gulls and cormorants: and in a dark tangle of chokecherry bushes, about two dozen nesting pairs of Black-crowned Night-Herons. "And young birds," she was quick to say: "They're of all different ages." She knew that this would be good news.

We met at dawn and paddled out in a misty drizzle to a great mound of an island clouded with about 10,000 Ring-billed Gulls, by Jackie's estimate; young bobbed on the water and adults swirled overhead as if around a hive. A corner of the island was dull black with cormorants, all waddling juveniles, and halfway up the slope were the chokecherries, from which now flew the herons, one by one, making off for the horizon in a straggling line. Before we'd even touched on shore, the last one flapped out and away with a disgruntled *vok*, unhappy at the unannounced disruption of a good day's sleep. A few Snowy Egrets followed.

We peered into their fortress. Sure enough, here were their beds of sticks, some on the ground but most placed (thoughtfully) about chest high, so that all one needed do was to lean in and hold back a branch or two. And there, crouched on their nests in fours and sometimes fives, were the most outlandish babies I had ever seen: some nearly naked and so young that they could hardly keep their heads up, but most fully pinfeathered, and formidable. One of these pinfeathered gangs was almost too good to believe: four bristling warriors, full of fight and not about to be intimidated. These goons I *had* to photograph.

At the sight of our white faces, all four heads shot up, mouths opened, and the rest of them ballooned like pufferfish, and when I leaned in close the near bird lunged and snapped his beak: whether to crush or skewer me with that blunt instrument, I wish I knew. With every lunge came a sharp nasal *jehk*, or *jahk*, only remotely like the *vok* one day to come.

We spelled each other, so that while the one held back a branch the other fired away; and it was a most frightful, wonderful tableau. That one nestful of lunatics alone was worth the drive.

What a madhouse, there, in that chokecherry thicket. What an island. We packed up the canoe and paddled off, our cameras full of pictures.

WOOD STORK
Mycteria americana

To see a rookery of wading birds you needn't clamber over mangrove roots and cypress knees, and wade among the snakes and alligators; so don't be deterred. Even a rookery of Wood Storks, birds known for nesting in the highest treetops: you can see one of the best by merely strolling down a boardwalk, without even changing out of your good shoes.

It's the Corkscrew Swamp Sanctuary, in Immokalee, Florida: a remnant grove of soaring 600-year-old bald cypresses, and home to the country's largest rookery of Wood Storks. For a small fee, you can wander through and ponder birds and trees alike in comfort, from a sturdy boardwalk.

In spring, the storks sail in with sticks grasped in their beaks and crash land at their nests high in the canopy, as Swallow-tailed Kites sail higher still, impassive in the blue, like giant butterflies. The stork numbers fluctuate from year to year, sometimes dramatically, depending on hydro cycles. In the 1930s, Corkscrew held 10,000 to 12,000 pairs of storks, but from 1967 through the early 1980s numbers fell by 75%. Nonetheless, in most years, Corkscrew's ancient cypresses still hold the largest colonies in North America.

Above:
(ADULT) – TAMPA BAY, FLORIDA, JUNE 2010
A crusty veteran, still at it: fishing by feel. On touching even the most minuscule of prey, its bill snaps shut in about 1/40 of a second.

Right:
(YOUNG) – TAMPA BAY, FLORIDA, JUNE 2010
One parent is always posted at the nest to guard against rogue non-breeding storks, which may destroy the eggs and young of mated pairs.

CANADA GEESE (YOUNG) – CHURCHILL, MANITOBA, JULY 2011

III

Ducklings, Goslings: The Little Dears

TO SOME BIRD ENTHUSIASTS, THE DUCKS ARE A DULL LOT: BALL-HEADED, PLUMP, UNMUSICAL (TO SAY THE LEAST), AND ALL TOO VISIBLE; TOO "EASY." When out bobbing on the open water, and without a wisp of grass or sedge or reed within a quarter mile, they have no more mystique than cattle lounging on a pasture.

The *ducklings*, on the other hand—who can resist the fuzzy ducklings? The big baby eyes and rubber-ducky bills, and molded-rubber "smiles"? Ducklings are sympathetic creatures, at once playful, curious, and vulnerable. We feel for the ducklings.

Like all "precocials," they are self-sufficient within hours of hatching, but they stay longer at the nest than most, and for good reason: to gain strength for the long march to water, soon to come. On command they all set off behind the mother, waddling and nudging, forging their way through and over the tough tangles of the prairie, sometimes for a mile or more: right up to the edges of their nursery pond and in, one sibling at a time.

And there they spend the next weeks swimming and exploring, snapping up small insects from the surface, and with luck eluding the bigger mouths that would snap them up. It could happen any moment, from above or below, and there wouldn't be a thing they could do but peep in protest.

A duckling doesn't know that, though, and he is always eager, always up for the adventure, wherever it may take him.

Above:
(YOUNG) – CHURCHILL, MANITOBA, JULY 2011
If you surprise a lone gosling up close, it will not run, but freeze. So much does it trust in its camouflage that you could pick it up and bite it, and I'll bet it wouldn't budge.

Right:
(ADULT AND YOUNG) – CHURCHILL, MANITOBA, JULY 2011

CANADA GOOSE
Branta canadensis

Beyond my boyhood yard in Massachusetts, just a minute's walk away, lay a Great Plains. They were a place to play, to throw a boomerang perhaps or to hit and shag fly balls, at least when not usurped by the relentless golfers, who played through as if they owned the place (they did); but they were not a place for birds. Aside from a few roving crows and robins, and sometimes an over-flying Red-tailed Hawk, all you could hope to see were herds of half-wild Canada Geese about the water hazards, milling on the water or out loafing on the fairway; and what oafs they were. What mockeries of wild, free-flying birds.

Yet people seemed to hold these birds in awe. "Few men have souls so dead that they will not bother to look up when they hear the barking of wild geese," wrote Roger Tory Peterson, and I was moved by his plainspoken poignancy; but why? What in the world was so soul-stirring in these big oafs of the golf course? To me they were no less domesticated than the golfers, and about as interesting.

The trouble was that having seen only my golf course geese, I didn't know that there could be any others. It was not until one crisp October day years later, at the mouth of the Connecticut River, that I first heard the "barking of wild geese"; and so high were they in the clear, thin air that even with binoculars I had to strain to see them.

Back in the days of the frontier, a "giant" race of Canada Goose, *Branta canadensis maxima*, still bred in the interior of North America, from central Manitoba southward to Kentucky, but like any wildlife within reach of shooting, it was shot, and by the early 1900s it had been driven nearly to extinction. But before that happened, some of the big birds were bred in captivity, and

CANADA GEESE (YOUNG) – CHURCHILL, MANITOBA, JULY 2011

their wild population was eventually "reestablished," no doubt to preserve the "resource" for the very ones who'd done the decimating; and so well did this feral population thrive that it has since spread well beyond the bird's original breeding range.

Those geese have now become a population of non-migratory nuisance birds. By the late 1900s, the numbers of the giant Canadas had so increased in some states, especially in urban areas—Minneapolis alone had some 27,000 by 1988—that the USDA began to "cull" them. Not only were these nuisance geese attacking people and their poodles, and endangering air traffic (remember the Sully Sullenberger plane of 2008, downed in the Hudson when geese clogged its engines?), but their high-volume pooping was eutrophicating ponds and lakes and fouling lawns and schoolyards, parks, and playing fields—and golf courses.

So there was all the difference in the world between the oaf birds of my golf course and the wild high-fliers of the North. It would take a while—more than half a century, in fact—but one day I would see the North from which those "real" geese came.

In late June and July at Churchill, Manitoba, on the western shores of Hudson Bay, they dominate the landscape like no other bird. Along the gravel road from town, you meet with traffic not of vehicles but of geese, pairs crossing with straw-yellow broods in tow, all heading west from their inland nesting grounds to their brood-rearing commons on salt marshes, up to two miles away.

Should you run up to intercept one of these families, as might a hungry fox or polar bear, the goslings will slip in to hide behind the nearest parent, and the parent will stand fast: wings spread and neck outstretched, mouth open, hissing at you like a serpent. I'll bet that if you ran right up and tried to grab a gosling, the old bird would strike you.

But even these, the wild high-fliers of the North, can pose environmental problems. The problem here at Churchill is the impact their foraging has on the wet sedge meadow and tundra habitat of nesting Dunlins and other shorebird species. In the summer of 2011, vast tracts were goose-chomped to the very mud, and the mud itself was fouled with the real thing: wild northern goose poop.

Above and right:
(YOUNG) – CRANE LAKE, SASKATCHEWAN, JULY 1995
First try?

AMERICAN WIGEON
Anas americana

I was up to my belly in Crane Lake, Saskatchewan, pushing the blind along and taking in the beauty of the evening—the blue water and the golden hills beyond, the Marsh Wrens chattering and Yellow-headed Blackbirds braying from the reeds—when a dull yellow duckling glided out into the open. He was 30 feet away or more, but I framed him up, and as I reached to focus he stood straight up on the water, buzzed his stubby wings—I fired—and then he fell back belly-down on the water, like a proper duckling.

It wouldn't be much of a photograph. Not only was the chick too distant, but my camera was entirely manual and the lens was of the old twist-to-focus type, so there was no time to pause and contemplate, check shutter speed and aperture, or even focus carefully: I had to hit the button *now*, or never. And how could I not? This stand-up-on-the-water trick was irresistible, and almost unbelievable; for what I couldn't see was what he had beneath the surface: two big paddle feet. It was a moment not to miss.

What kind of duckling was it? I would have had no idea, had not the mother bird appeared some yards beyond, at once providing my lone duckling with a name: it was a Blue-winged Teal.

I thought so for the longest time, and gave it not another thought. The female Blue-wing was the only other duck out on the lake that evening, and she lingered, looking on with what could only be solicitude; so what else could the little fellow be? It was a Blue-winged Teal, and that was that; and so it would remain for nearly twenty years. But then it fell before the eye of Ian Gereg, a waterfowl biologist who knows the plumages of ducklings like no other, and he

told me what I might have found out on my own if I had done my homework: that my downy Blue-winged Teal was not a Blue-winged Teal at all, but an American Wigeon. He'd saved my lazy neck.

In fact, the downy wigeon is one of the more distinctive of North American ducklings, if only for its indistinctness. Unlike most downies of the freshwater "pond" ducks, or "dabblers," it is dull yellow overall, with none of the bold facial marks so prevalent in the other species: no dark cheek patch, crown stripe, or stripe through the eye, and no white patches on the wings or body. It has no markings anywhere, essentially, and nothing more to distinguish it than a light yellow eye ring and two other, even subtler features better left to experts such as Gereg: a "short, slightly tapered bill" and a "rather trapezoidal head shape."[*]

In any case, I should have done some homework. I'd assumed my duckling was a teal because there was a teal nearby, and I knew better than to do that, really. You can't tell a duckling by the company it keeps, because ducks are notorious for laying their eggs in the nests of other ducks. It happens all the time, and there's a name for it: "brood parasitism."[†] A chick in line behind a mother Gadwall might be not a Gadwall but a Canvasback or Redhead, and the chick behind a Redhead hen might be a Gadwall.

I'd known all that. But then along had come this female Teal, and I thought that I could take the easy way. I had *assumed*.

[*] Colleen Helgeson Nelson, *The Downy Waterfowl of North America* (1995).

[†] For more on this phenomenon, see Redhead (page 89).

AMERICAN WIGEON (ADULT) - CAMBRIDGE, MARYLAND, MARCH 2011

LESSER SCAUP
Aythya affinis

Lesser Scaup, Greater Scaup; tweedle-dee, tweedle-dum. They are near look-alikes, it's true, but one is far the more appealing—this, the Lesser—and it all has to do with head shape.

The Greater's head is neat, symmetrical, round as a ball, and the Lesser's out-of-round, imperfect, with a nice jaunty upswing at the rear, and that one touch makes all the difference. It's the difference between one's lively, pert expression and that of a dullard.

The Lesser duckling is a lively character, too, drab though it is. It's olive brown above, and buffy brown below and on the face, with no distinctive field marks whatsoever other than a faint line through the eye: the perfect anatid equivalent of one of Roger Tory Peterson's "confusing fall warblers."

"A 'confusing fall warbler' of the prairie ponds," he might have called it. But what energy. The duckling in the photograph swam back and forth before the blind for an hour or more, head darting and bill jabbing at the water constantly to snap up bits too small to see; and every ten or fifteen seconds, suddenly, with no sign of what was to come—no tilt-back of the head, no pause, no arching of the back, not so much as a squint or a twinkle of the eye—he jumped up like a toad, plunged in headfirst, and disappeared. Then he bobbed up again and swam on blithely as before, as if the interruption hadn't happened.

He was alone on a small North Dakota pond, without a single sibling in the world, but he didn't seem to know, or care. He was too busy.

The Lesser Scaup doesn't breed until its second year, and it seems fitting that this tot should have an extra year to buzz about the sloughs wherever

Above and right:
(YOUNG) – TOWNER COUNTY, NORTH DAKOTA, JULY 2010

whimsy takes him, enjoying life as a boy. But there's another, scientific explanation for that busyness.

A duckling needs the company of other ducklings, and without them it can't function as it should: so wrote the ornithologist Margaret Morse Nice, citing the case of a "small Velvet Scoter, lost from its mother and brothers and sisters," that was "constantly in motion and [could] not stop to feed or preen or rest."

She wrote also of a newly hatched Mallard duckling placed in a box with two slightly older Redheads. Though the Redheads attacked it constantly, every time the tiny Mallard was withdrawn to safety it called out in dismay until it was returned to the box with its "tormentors."

East vs. West

Heaven knows why ducks should be so much more wary on the East Coast than the West.

"At Merritt Lake, in Oakland," wrote Roger Tory Peterson, "I have had wild pintails and canvasbacks take bread and popcorn from my fingers. But along the Atlantic seaboard, I am doing well if I can approach a canvasback within a hundred yards, or in some places, a quarter of a mile."

We easterners do have a "Merritt Lake," of sorts: at Cambridge, Maryland, where an old seawall fronts on the Choptank River. In winter, several hundred ducks of half a dozen species can be found close to shore, milling about and waiting for cracked corn to be tossed in by local residents. The two most common: Canvasbacks and Lesser Scaup.

Above:
LESSER SCAUP (YOUNG) – TOWNER COUNTY, NORTH DAKOTA, JULY 2010

Left:
LESSER SCAUP (ADULT) – CAMBRIDGE, MARYLAND, MARCH 2011

"Surface Gleaning"

The mayfly in this photograph was striving to break free of its exuvia, unfold its wings for the first time, and fly; but fly it never would. Had the camera shutter fired one millisecond later, that mayfly wouldn't be there.

But the story of this mayfly isn't as sad as it sounds, for, like other aquatic insects in their nymph stage, it had already lived most of its natural life in the dim nether regions of the pond. For a year or two, even three, it enjoyed the fulfilling high life of a naiad: prowling, browsing the mud along the bottom, climbing and investigating rootstalks and sedge stems, or just flipping about the water column on its paddle tail, like a micro-miniature dolphin. When it surfaces at last, sloughs off its jacket and emerges to become a winged free spirit of the air, it has only a day or two, a few at most, in which to mate, lay eggs, and die.

The mayfly is but one of many small invertebrates that throng the North Dakota ponds. Throughout the Prairie Pothole region, some 10 million ducklings every year depend upon a bounty of emerging mayflies, midges, caddis flies, and a wide range of other insects and crustacea, including earthworms, fairy shrimp and clam shrimp, seed shrimp, water fleas, and nymphs of dragonflies and damselflies.

Diving and dabbling ducks alike—scaup, Redheads and Canvasbacks, and Mallards, Gadwalls, pintails, teals, and shovelers—in their first weeks on the prairie ponds, all ducklings thrive on this vast host of invertebrates.

GADWALL (YOUNG) – TOWNER COUNTY, NORTH DAKOTA, JULY 2010
Fixed in the duckling's beady stare, a mere snap of the bill away:
an emerging mayfly, or ephemerid.

NORTHERN SHOVELER
Anas clypeata

The bill is the distinctive feature, of course, and it's distinctive in not only form, but function. This bill is designed for feeding in the way of a right whale.

Just as the whale strains seawater through plates of baleen to extract zooplankton, a Northern Shoveler plows through the shallows of a prairie pond to strain out its food: mostly the minute crustaceans known as *cladocerans*, or water fleas, but also a wide range of other small invertebrates, and even seeds. The straining structure in its bill, not unlike the whale's baleen, comprises rows of narrow comb-like teeth, known as *lamellae*. Other surface-feeding ducks have their lamellae, but only in the shoveler are they so well developed, and so pronounced that you can plainly see them, even when the bill is closed.

A shoveler duckling doesn't screen its food through lamellae, though; it feeds by "surface gleaning" (page 78). Like other ducklings on the pond, it simply swims and scans the surface, scooping up whatever small prey it can find.

Above:
(ADULT, DRAKE) – STUTSMAN COUNTY, NORTH DAKOTA, JUNE 2013

Left:
(YOUNG) – TOWNER COUNTY, NORTH DAKOTA, JUNE 2011
In its first two weeks, a "spoonbill" (as the hunters call it) may look like any other dabbler duckling. But then the snout becomes apparent, and there's no mistaking it.

Above:
NORTHERN SHOVELER (ADULT, HEN) – TOWNER COUNTY, NORTH DAKOTA, JULY 2011

Left:
NORTHERN SHOVELER (ADULT, DRAKE) – STUTSMAN, NORTH DAKOTA, JULY 2010

NORTHERN SHOVELER (ADULT AND YOUNG) –
TOWNER COUNTY, NORTH DAKOTA, JUNE 2011

(ADULT AND YOUNG) – BARROW, ALASKA, JULY 2013
The duckling's "spectacles," as you can see, are dark brown patches outlined by light brown crescents.
The adult male's are bright white "goggles" on a darker, greenish face, and the female's—usually—are light brown against a darker brown: a "pale ghost image of the 'goggles,'" as Roger Tory Peterson so neatly put it. But not this female's, oddly: her spectacles are darker brown than the surrounding face.

SPECTACLED EIDER
Somateria fischeri

The question had bedeviled scientists for more than a century: where do these birds winter? After a brief nesting season on the tundra of northern Alaska and eastern Russia, and then a month or two spent molting in the offshore waters of the Bering Sea, the entire world population of Spectacled Eiders vanished from the map, not to be seen again until they reappeared on their breeding grounds in May.

Where did they go? The mystery persisted until March 1995, when a freak signal received from a long-inactive radio transmitter inspired biologists to conduct aerial searches of the frozen Bering Sea southwest of St. Lawrence Island. What they found was something like 150,000 Spectacled Eiders, packed by the tens of thousands into holes kept open by the birds themselves, all within a 20-square-mile area; and later surveys turned up something like a quarter of a million: roughly, the entire world population. The sea around them was a boundless, lifeless waste of white, and the temperature -20° F. But on the ocean floor, 120 to 300 feet below, lay what sustained them: a vast smorgasbord of clams, marine worms, and crustaceans.

These eider concentrations have been likened to the spectacle of wintering monarch butterflies in the mountain forests north of Mexico City. Indeed, one body-to-body flock alone held more than 30,000 eiders.

On their breeding grounds, the eiders do not dive to such great depths to pluck clams from the sea bed. They feed in tundra pools no more than five or six feet deep, and much of what they eat is on or near the surface: insects, insect larvae, and other small invertebrates.

Like its companion phalaropes and jaegers, the Spectacled Eider is another arctic sea bird that resides upon the tundra only briefly, and only because it has to: it needs solid ground on which to nest. And once done with its nesting, it wastes little time in leaving. The pair arrives in May, and within weeks, before the female has even begun to incubate her clutch of eggs, the male vamooses and returns to the sea. He spends *eleven* months a year at sea, and the female, who alone cares for the eggs and young, spends eight or nine at sea.

The ducklings, like all ducklings, are precocial prodigies. Within a day or two of hatching, they can walk, feed, even swim; and by the end of August, twelve weeks later, they can fly. By early September— just as the tundra pools begin to freeze—young birds and mother birds take off together for their molting and staging areas offshore.

After molting they take off again, the entire population, for their distant winter haven in the Bering Sea south of St. Lawrence Island. By mid-November, they are gone without a trace.

DUCKLINGS, GOSLINGS: THE LITTLE DEARS

REDHEAD
Aythya americana

How to identify a duckling? The problem is a sticky one for even the most practiced waterfowl biologist, and it's made all the stickier by hens who take the easy way to nesting: brood parasitism.

For most birds, you can reasonably presume a downy chick to be the progeny of the adult bird nearest it, and most anxious for its safety; but not when it comes to ducklings. A duckling in tow behind a mother Gadwall, for example, is *probably* a Gadwall, but you can't be sure; it might also be the offspring of a shiftless Canvasback or Redhead.

The trouble is that many hens would just as soon avoid the chore of nest building and all the bother and commitment to come with it; so they lay their eggs in nests of other ducks and slip away, leaving the rest to the unwitting foster parents. The practice is especially common among Redheads, Canvasbacks, and Ruddies, but all duck species—and even the odd coot or grebe or Sora— have been found guilty. The resulting "dump nest" may contain the eggs of not just two but three or even four or more duck species.

So while chances are that every chick behind that mother Gadwall is a Gadwall, you never know. The duckling hatching in the nest at left will one day—if it is a male— have a bright red head.

Left:
(YOUNG) – TOWNER COUNTY, NORTH DAKOTA, JULY 2011
In a year, about half of these dull yellow ducklings will be dull brown hens.
The other half—the drakes—will have red heads.

Above:
(YOUNG) – AUDUBON NWR, NORTH DAKOTA, JUNE 2012
Whose duckling is it? In a nest full of white Gadwall eggs, one bluish egg—and an emerging Redhead. The Redhead is said to be more given to "brood parasitism" than any other North American duck.

REDHEAD (YOUNG) – TOWNER COUNTY, NORTH DAKOTA, JULY 2010

REDHEAD (ADULT) – CAMBRIDGE, MARYLAND, MARCH 2012

(JUVENILE) – TOWNER COUNTY, NORTH DAKOTA, AUGUST 2010

RUDDY DUCK
Oxyura jamaicensis

Even the drab winter-plumaged bird has its appeal, with its big head, Donald-Ducky bill, and wren-like tail; but you don't really know the Ruddy Duck until you've seen the drake in spring on a blue North Dakota pool, adrift among the rushes with tail up, flanks ruddy chestnut, and a bill of baby blue that looks like it was freshly dipped in paint.

The Ruddy is an odd duck. Its legs, like those of grebes, are placed so far astern that they are all but useless when on land; and even takeoff from water is a struggle, for it has to skip along for tens of yards, wings buzzing and feet pattering like mad, before at last becoming airborne.

Its eggs, too. They are so large that they have passed for eggs of ducks three times its size: the much larger Canvasback's, for instance, whose eggs are actually *smaller* than the Ruddy's. One recorded clutch of 14 Ruddy eggs, laid over a span of 14 days, weighed three pounds: three times the weight of the poor hen that laid them.

The newly hatched Ruddy is among the most precocious of the ducklings, and can swim and dive on its first contact with water. When captive-bred chicks have been experimentally released on hatching, they have simply raised themselves.

Cute as a button though they are, they are the feistiest of ducklings. One three-day-old chick chased after an entire brood of two-week-old Mallards, and when at last the Mallards turned on him, he bit them.

(ADULT AND YOUNG) – TOWNER COUNTY, NORTH DAKOTA, AUGUST 2010
Among her dozen ducklings, a hen Ruddy sits stone-still at the photographer's approach, eyes glaring and neck elevated like a periscope: a live hair-trigger, ready at the first false move to send young splashing every which way. But she does not. In time, she grows accustomed to the blind.

Above and right:
RUDDY DUCKS (YOUNG) – TOWNER COUNTY, NORTH DAKOTA, AUGUST 2010
This is the feistiest of ducklings. When just a few hours old, a hand-held Ruddy chick is apt to snap, peck, and bite a person's fingers.

The "Bubbling" Display

A drake Ruddy swims with head held high and a chin-up cocky look, as if he owns the place. But when he displays to the females and you hear him quack, you'll want to laugh out loud.

He glides along in style when suddenly, as if seized in a fit, he bobs his head up and down like a sewing machine, his bill smacking the water and his breast, and out come sputtered quacks that sound like a kazoo, or a tin horn under water.

Above:
RUDDY DUCKS (ADULT AND YOUNG) – TOWNER COUNTY, NORTH DAKOTA, AUGUST 2010

Left:
RUDDY DUCK (ADULT) – SIDEWOOD, SASKATCHEWAN, JULY 2012
Unlike other drakes, decked out in their full-color glory by October or November and on through the winter, the Ruddy doesn't molt into his fancy courtship colors until April—more like a songbird than a duck.

LONG-TAILED DUCKS (ADULT AND YOUNG) – BARROW, ALASKA, JULY 2012

RUDDY DUCKS (JUVENILE) – TOWNER COUNTY, NORTH DAKOTA, AUGUST 2010

COMMON GALLINULES (JUVENILE) – PALM BEACH COUNTY, FLORIDA, APRIL 2009

IV

The Ugly Duckling: Mud Hens

COULD A BABY BE LESS GIFTED THAN ONE OF THESE FRUMPY YOUNGSTERS?

They are the young of rails and coots and gallinules—the *Rallidae*, or "mud hens" as they're known colloquially, and they could hardly be more homely. Their down is black, their bodies tubby and heads nearly neckless, yet they fuss about so busily and cheerfully that you might think they knew already of their coming frogs-to-princes transformation.

One mud hen in particular: you won't believe the shining prince that it becomes.

Most *Rallidae* keep out of sight among the cattails, sedges, and *Spartina* grasses, but not coots and gallinules; they take to the open marsh-ringed ponds and marshes mixed with open water, where they can alternately swim and walk upon the vegetation. So you might see a mother and her train of babies stepping over lotus pads, like rails, or in over their bellies swimming, like a family of ducks.

(ADULT) – TOWNER COUNTY, NORTH DAKOTA, AUGUST 2010

AMERICAN COOT
Fulica americana

On the Northern Plains, you'd be hard pressed to find a single marsh-ringed pond or pool not animated by a pair or two of coots, and you'd have no trouble seeing them. Unlike their wily relatives the rails, they hardly keep themselves a secret.

Coots are the clown birds of the sloughs, always yakking, skirmishing, or otherwise making a production of themselves. They make an ordeal even of the act of swimming, pumping their heads and croaking as they go, as if that should increase their speed, and they express the same impatience when they're feeding and the sedges don't tear off as quickly as they ought to. Or when the neighbors stray in too close for their liking: the contenders clash in splashy scuffles, until one or the other is chased off the premises.

Splashing—that's another kooky thing about the coots. They do it all the time: when feeding, and when scuffling, and when making their long pitter-patter takeoffs from the water. Indeed, an old-time nickname for the coot is "splatterer."

The downy coot is a "fantastic looking creature," in the words of one orni-thologist*; and in another's words† it is "grotesque but showy," a "black ball of down with a fiery head." Grotesque *and* showy: this Ugly Duckling is not only ugly, but bizarre. Yet those fantastic colors have been shown to serve a function: as a stimulus to parental feeding.

To see a brood of bobbing chicks strung out in disarray behind their par-

* Margaret Morse Nice
† Arthur Cleveland Bent

ents, or veering off as the breeze may take them, it's no surprise that many should be lost to predators. And it's no surprise that hens should lay so many eggs to compensate: ten or twelve per clutch on average, and in one case twenty-two.

The chick can swim and dive like an adult and stay submerged for nearly three minutes; but it's no match for a mink or Northern Harrier or Great Horned Owl. In June and July, as many a Plains biologist will tell you, the scat and pellets of these predators are often packed with bright red beaks.

(YOUNG) – SIDEWOOD, SASKATCHEWAN, JUNE 2012

THE UGLY DUCKLING: MUD HENS

AMERICAN COOT (ADULT) – TOWNER COUNTY, NORTH DAKOTA, AUGUST 2010

AMERICAN COOT (YOUNG) – TOWNER COUNTY, NORTH DAKOTA, AUGUST 2010

COMMON GALLINULE
Gallinula galeata

In the northeastern states, you seldom see a Common Gallinule, and if you do, you seldom get more than a rear-end glimpse as it slips off through the reeds. It's long been thought a shy bird of the wetland wilds, like a rail; but not all wetlands anymore are all that wild, and not all gallinules that shy. In some tame marshes of today, the gallinules parade as openly as chickens in a barnyard.

In southern Florida, for example: at the so-called Wakodahatchee Wetlands, a water treatment plant turned wildlife sanctuary in the heart of bustling Palm Beach County. At such peopled sites as this, the birds are often no more timid than the visitors.

The Common Gallinule is a prolific breeder. In the northern states, it raises two broods in a season, and in the south, three broods—so at about eight chicks per brood, that is a lot of gallinules. In Dade County, Florida, between March and September 1996, the biologist Brett Bannor took notes on a pair that raised not only three successive broods, or four, but *five*.

The chicks are jet-black urchins with heads bald and mangy-looking, as if the spray-on flocking had failed to cover. Except for the "fantastic"* coot chicks, there could be no Ugly Ducklings uglier than these; but if they have reason to be downcast, they don't seem to know. They are as alive and eager as bird babies anywhere.

And selfless: they pitch in to help their families in ways that you would not believe. When still just four or five weeks old, they actually help their parents feed and care for the chicks of later broods. And as if that were not sufficiently

---

* Margaret Morse Nice

beyond the call of duty for a month-old baby bird, they even help out with the nest building. The formal designation "juvenile helpers" hardly does them justice.

But that's not all they do. In another kind of family sharing, called "cooperative nesting," a young breeding female will move in to share a nest with her own mother, and help incubate *her* eggs as well as her own.

That's some cooperation.

Why Black?

Except for the coot's candy-red and orange on the head and neck, the down of all young "mud hens" (*Rallidae*) is uniformly black. The ornithologist Margaret M. Nice discovered why when she once tried to catch an escaped rail chick:

> *The value of the black plumage of these little rails was demonstrated to us when we lost a small Virginia Rail outdoors: as we searched through the grass we often snatched at shadows, convinced we were looking at our little bird.*

So they can pass for puffs of shadow: what better way to frustrate predators? A youngster could be worse than frumpy-looking, after all: it could be seen, and eaten.

COMMON GALLINULES (ADULT AND YOUNG) – PALM BEACH COUNTY, FLORIDA, APRIL 2009
The sharp spur on the young bird's "thumb" (or pollex) helps it clamber through the swampy jungle, both above the water and below. The bright red bill and frontal plate of the adult is thought to function as a stimulus, or releaser, prompting the chicks to beg for food.

PURPLE GALLINULE
Porphyrula martinica

The "Hen of Heaven," it's been called, and surely no bird is more heavenly. Not even that other rainbow-colored beauty of the South, the Painted Bunting.

And yet perhaps more stunning even than its colors is the chick's transformation from a coal-black mud hen: without a doubt, one of the most dramatic in the bird world. But then, none of the Ugly Duckling mud hen chicks is doomed to ugliness for long: not even the American Coot, and not the Common Gallinule. Within a year, they too emerge as handsome birds.

This Ugly Duckling—well, just wait until you see the beauty *it* becomes.

(YOUNG) – PALM BEACH COUNTY, FLORIDA, JUNE 2011

Where from the Colors?

In his journal entry for June 20, 1857, Henry David Thoreau quotes the words of a spellbound child first witnessing the flight song of a Bobolink: "What makes he sing so sweet, Mother? Do he eat flowers?"

Far be it from a gallinule to sing, of course, but this fantastic bird of marshes does eat flowers: in this case, the purple blossoms of fire flag. Would the same child have asked if that was how he got his *colors*?

The flowers, seeds, and other parts of various aquatic plants are a major part of the Purple Gallinule's diet.

PURPLE GALLINULE (ADULT) – PALM BEACH COUNTY, FLORIDA, JUNE 2011

BLACK TERNS (YOUNG) – TOWNER COUNTY, SOUTH DAKOTA, JUNE 2011
The long, tawny down distinguishes it at once from the whitish young of other terns. The white frames on the face, too,
will identify the Black Tern chick; but they fade away soon after its fledged.

V

Sea Wings: Gulls & Terns, etc.

THESE ARE THE WHITE BIRDS OF THE SEASHORE, AS FAMILIAR AS THE WHITE OF SAILS, AND GRACEFUL, ALWAYS, IN THE AIR AND ON THE WATER. And on picture postcards, placemats, and watercolor seascapes hanging on the wall.

That's one way to picture them, but there's another.

To picture **gulls**, real gulls, picture a mass of mobbing, squabbling opportunists; and picture leavings: refuse heaps, and offal strewn from fishing boats, black plastic garbage bags and dumpsters, and McDonald's parking lots. Like rats, most gulls are creatures not of the wild free spaces but of the fouled, the artificial, and the urban, indeed almost any peopled space as long as there are easy pickings to be had. The gulls are tough, adaptable, resourceful, no doubt about it—and "successful," like the teeming species they so readily depend upon.

There are exceptions: Franklin's Gull, for one, the "prairie pigeon" of the Northern Plains. You won't likely catch the Franklin's grubbing about in dumps or dumpsters: not on its breeding grounds, at least, though a few have been so tempted on migration. It is an admirable gull.

The **terns** are sharp-winged, sharp-billed variations on the gulls, with black caps (usually) and notched tails. They do not sail in flight like gulls, but power through the air with strong, deep-rowing strokes; indeed they are in all ways more assertive, more a family of go-getters. Whereas a gull is all too pleased to snap up anything that comes its way—somebody else's catch, scraps tossed from a fishing boat, or something washed up at the wrack line—a tern would rather find its own prey, thank you, and would rather that it be alive.

Even on their breeding grounds, most gulls are rather passive, almost indifferent to intrusion; but not terns, not by a long shot. They are irascible, high-strung, and quick to anger at the slightest provocation.

BLACK TERN (YOUNG) – TOWNER COUNTY, SOUTH DAKOTA, JUNE 2011
At first glance it appears gentle and refined, like a prim lady taking tea. But look again—at the hard eyes,
and the sharp snatching bill—and it no longer seems so civilized.

If you've ever wandered too close to a colony, you know with what ferocity they rise to swoop and scream at you, repeatedly, until you've beat a full retreat. And if you don't retreat—or heaven forbid, you dare to step even closer—you know that you'll be subjected to not only screaming but attack by strafing: first with their bills, and then with well-aimed rounds of excrement.

Young terns and gulls are neither precocial nor altricial, but *semi-precocial*. Like precocial species, they can walk and swim soon after hatching, but like altricial birds they cannot feed themselves.

Two other skillful fliers, not closely related to the gulls or terns, but both far-ranging birds of oceans, are the **Northern Gannet** and the **Long-tailed Jaeger**. The gannet breeds in colonies of many thousands on Atlantic sea cliffs, and the jaeger nests among the shorebirds of the arctic tundra.

(YOUNG) – PERCÉ, QUEBEC, JULY 2012

NORTHERN GANNET
Morus bassanus

This big bird is a show-stopper in several ways, but most impressively of all, perhaps, in its performance as a self-directing missile. It's the plunge-diving fisherman *par excellence.*

When the herring, capelin, or mackerel are schooling and word gets out, as if by cellphone, the gannets gather by the hundreds, hover, get a fix on the fish below, and the attack begins. One by one the birds fold up their wings, and down they go, bill first into the sea like raining arrows, and if need be they propel themselves like penguins to a depth of 40 feet or more, snap up their prey, and often swallow it before resurfacing.

In search of schooling fish, they routinely range a hundred miles or more from the nesting colonies.

Another spectacle is posed by the sheer numbers of the bright white birds strewn all across their nesting ledges, like confetti. At last count, in 2012, the colony at Bonaventure Island in Quebec held 51,700 pairs of birds. That's *pairs* of birds: or better than 100,000 breeding birds. Of the six major colonies in North America, Bonaventure's is the largest.

Like other seabirds, gannets nest in colonies on ledges of colossal sea cliffs and sea islands, often hundreds of feet above the surf, where they are safe from all but the most foolhardy of predators. But you can see one of their colonies with ease, pain-free, for the cost of a boat ride; and it's the big one: at Bonaventure.

To see the gannets at their busiest, when the young are in the nests, plan a visit in the first three weeks of July. Make the interminable drive up the

(ADULT) – PERCÉ, QUEBEC, JULY 2012

Gaspé to Percé, pay the parking lot manager for passage on the charter boat, and line up at the wharf, embark, be seated and enjoy the ride, but don't relax; observe. The boat loops out around the north end of the island, past the most titanic cliff face you have ever seen, or will see, and a grand gallery of seabirds: not only a considerable percentage of the island's gannets, but 34,454 Common Murres (the latest count, from 2008) and 16,400 Black-legged Kittiwakes (2013), to name just some. They sit on their home ledges, tier upon tier: birds by the tens of thousands, all lined up and looking out to sea, like city high-rise dwellers from their porches on a steamy weekend afternoon. Murres and other alcids buzz by overhead on forays out to sea and back, and one of the interpreters aboard will tell you which are which—in English, if you please. Others nesting on the ledges include Double-crested and Great Cormorants, Razorbills, Black Guillemots, Herring and Great Black-backed Gulls, and a few opportunist Common Ravens, and Bald Eagles. But the main spectacle is yet to come: on top.

The boat continues out around the island, and then docks. After disembarking, you set off on a stiff forty-minute hike, up all the way until you reach a fenced-off ledge, 250 feet above the sea; and here the gannets come and go, sit on their round mud nests and tend their nestlings, only one young to the pair. The nests are ugly, slovenly affairs, but around each one is a respectfully maintained two- to three-foot space. The young themselves are not so lovely either, with their crinkled, vulturesque black faces. Vulturesque: that really is the word.

After ninety days, the young are ready. *Ninety* days: that's a long time for young birds to be on the ground and helpless to escape; it's no small wonder that their colonies require an island fortress beyond reach of the large mammal predators.

At ninety days, the youngster makes its way to the precipice, takes a few trial flaps, and off it goes, falling and gliding and half-flying out for several hundred yards and down, inexorably; then it lands with a splash, and swims on out to sea. Of the young birds in the months to come, when they learn to fly and feed, little is known.

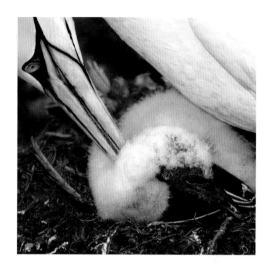

Above and left:
NORTHERN GANNET (ADULT AND YOUNG) – PERCÉ, QUEBEC, JULY 2012
The nest mound of the gannet is composed of mud and poop and feathers, grass, and flotsam, but that isn't always all. Sometimes it tosses in such ornamental doodads as false teeth, a gold watch or fountain pen, golf balls, a length of plastic rope, even a catheter: all have been found in the mud nests of gannets.

SEA WINGS: GULLS & TERNS, ETC.

Above:
(ADULT) – SIDEWOOD, SASKATCHEWAN, JULY 2012
A Franklin's nesting colony, wrote Arthur Cleveland Bent in his Life Histories, "is one of the most spectacular, most interesting, and most beautiful sights in the realm of North American ornithology. The man who has never seen one has something yet to live for. . . ."

Right:
(YOUNG) – CRANE LAKE, SASKATCHEWAN, JULY 2007

FRANKLIN'S GULL
Leucophaeus pipixcan

Unlike its black-hooded alter ego in the East, the Laughing Gull, you won't find this gull grubbing about in dumps or the dumpsters in McDonald's parking lots: not on its breeding grounds, at least.

The Franklin's is the wild gull, emblem of the rolling plains and open skies, and the prairie lakes it seeks out for its nesting. You're apt to see its loose flocks anywhere on the Northern Plains, racing past low in the wind, wings raked, or wheeling in the tranquil blue, so high sometimes that all you see is their white glints; or bobbing in the sloughs, benign and smooth as dolls. This is *the* gull of the prairies.

A Franklin's nesting colony is an exhilarating sight. The wild cries, the adults swirling overhead; the young birds peering from their nests, and drifting on the water—the scene is dizzying, almost overwhelming.

The nestlings often scuttle off the nests too soon and swim away, eager to see some of the big new world of water, and they sail off weightlessly upon the slightest breeze, much to the fury of their parents, which swoop down and seize them by the neck and fling them back in the direction of the nest: repeatedly, if necessary, until they are returned—if not each to its own nest, at least to some nest.

The poor chicks are left chastened and bedraggled, exhausted, and sometimes even bleeding from their parents' pecks and pinches.

BLACK TERN
Chlidonias niger

The Black Tern builds its floating nests in colonies, like certain grebes, but its colonies are smaller: seldom of more than a dozen pairs.

A *floating* nest is suited to the all-aquatic grebes, but to a tern? No other tern except the Forster's will nest over water, and that species' nest requires some kind of solid substrate, like a clod of floating peat or a muskrat house. But when you think of it, what better way to frustrate predators? Not many foxes or raccoons would choose to flounder through four feet of cattail-stubbled water on the off chance of a set of eggs or young birds. For a photographer, on the other hand: what an *opportunity*. What better than a brood of wide-eyed young marooned and waiting on a floating platter, with no place to go? It would be almost too easy.

All I had to do was find one of those floating nests with downy young, then move in with a floating blind and camera. Right?

Not right. I spent a morning in a North Dakota slough among these terns, and picked out sites to which I'd seen the adults bringing food; and each time I approached one in the blind I found the floating nest, all right—but it was empty. There was not a chick in sight.

Were these birds playing games with me?

Young gulls and terns alike, I learned, are not bound to their nests, like hawks and herons. They are *semi-precocial*, which is to say that though fed by their parents, they are free to leave the nest at any time. So if a predator appears and the adults sound the alarm, the chicks scuttle off, swim ten or fifteen yards, and crouch beneath the cattails until danger passes. Only after many minutes,

Above:
(YOUNG) – TOWNER COUNTY, NORTH DAKOTA, JUNE 2011
The long, tawny down distinguishes it at once from the whitish young of other terns. The white frames on the face, too, will identify the Black Tern chick; but they fade away soon after it has fledged.

Left:
(ADULT) – TOWNER COUNTY, NORTH DAKOTA, JUNE 2011
Stay back, or the sharp yips of protest will give way to screams of white-hot fury, and that hard, sharp bill will rap you on the noggin.
The Black Tern doesn't plunge into the water for its prey like other terns, but hawks and snatches it in flight. And unlike others, it will take not only fish but dragonflies and damselflies, mayflies, moths and beetles, spiders, grasshoppers, and even crayfish and small mollusks.

when the adults call out the wheezy notes of the "all clear," do they return to their home bases.

It took a while, but I figured out their game, and set out in the blind to try again . . . but differently. I snuck in very, very slowly, making maybe thirty feet in half an hour, hoping to catch a brood of young at home. It worked, and what I found were three brown suntanned-looking downies, relaxed and peering at me through what might have been the chic white frames of sunglasses.

They might have been three suntanned teens, sprawled out and lounging by the pool while Mom was away rounding up the drinks and chips.

Above and left:
BLACK TERN (ADULT AND YOUNG) – TOWNER COUNTY, NORTH DAKOTA, JUNE 2011
By this time the photographer was tiring, too—and cold, having waded chest-deep in a North Dakota slough for about five hours.

Above:
(ADULT) – CHURCHILL, MANITOBA, JULY 2011
The distance champion: In another month it will leave its breeding grounds on Hudson Bay to embark on a winding oceanic journey all the way to the seas of Antarctica, only to return again in spring: in all, a pole-to-pole-to-pole round trip thought to total nearly 50,000 miles per year—the longest made by any creature on the planet.

Right:
(YOUNG) – CHURCHILL, MANITOBA, JULY 2011
You can tell it from the chicks of other terns by its large charcoal bib, which extends almost to the eyes and surrounds the base of the bill.

ARCTIC TERN
Sterna paradisaea

No tern is fiercer in defending its nesting ground. If a potential predator comes gliding in by air, a Raven or a Glaucous Gull, let's say, the terns will rise up as a body and give chase and mob it mercilessly, swooping down and striking from behind. In Alaska, a Bald Eagle was so fiercely mobbed by Arctic Terns that it was driven down into the water, and had to *swim* ashore to safety.

And when the threat is posed by an intruding mammal—you, let's say—the response is much the same. At your approach, they rise in pairs and hover overhead, and snap out a single *tik* note at forbearing intervals of several seconds: *tik . . . tik . . . tik . . . ;* but they are not forbearing long. If you persist, the *tiks* will quicken, and if you still persist the birds will swoop, scream bloody murder and attack you, with sharp bill raps on the head. And if you *still* persist, they strike again, letting go with well-aimed missiles.

If you didn't know already, you might wonder what the fuss was all about, for the pale waste about you looks as vacant as a moonscape. But it's not, of course. It holds their nests, if you could call them that, and in the nests are eggs, or chicks: in either case, all but invisible against the sand and stone.

If they are chicks, and they hear parents screeching overhead, they hunker down and wait. Or they shuffle off the nest for a few yards, then hunker down and wait: and when the screeching stops, they shuffle back again.

LONG-TAILED JAEGER
Stercorarius longicaudus

I'd seen my first Long-tailed Jaeger earlier that very day, streaming low over the Barrow tundra, so you can imagine my surprise when I walked into Sam and Lee's for supper and the first thing that I saw, pinned on the wall beside the inner door, was a photo of a boy wearing a hat—and on top of the hat, plain as you please, a Long-tailed Jaeger.

"Who took that *photo*?" I asked my waitress.

"Oh, you like photography," she said with a pleased smile. "You'll have to meet Floyd!" Her name was Lee, and the boy in the photograph was Ben, her ten-year-old.

She reached for a phone, still smiling, and before I'd finished with my dinner salad, he was there, the Ancient Mariner himself, facing me through beard from straight across the booth: Floyd Davidson, a "cranky old man," as he describes himself, but a photographer as well. He had more high-tech digital equipment with him in the booth than I'd know what to do with.

"I'll take you there tonight," he said. "Finish up your dinner—go ahead, take your time—and I'll see you back here at nine." The warm summer light at nine PM at Barrow, I had to remind myself—the locals enjoy pointing out that you're inside the Arctic Circle—is about like that of a late summer afternoon in Massachusetts.

The week before, Floyd told me, he and Ben had buzzed out on the tundra on his ATV, past the town dump and on to a point looking out on the Arctic Ocean, and no sooner had they stepped down from the ATV than this big bird flew in, swooped down and circled, and set down gently on Ben's head. And Floyd, his camera ready, took one dandy of a picture. "There had to be a nest or

(YOUNG) – BARROW, ALASKA, JULY 2012
Within a day or two of hatching, the young jaeger toddles off to hide. Before embarking on its maiden flight some 25 days later, it might have toddled off 500 yards or more from the nest site.

young nearby," he said. Floyd may not have known it was a Long-tailed, but he knew it was a jaeger, and he knew what made it tick. And sure enough, after a search of the surrounding grasses, he had found the chick.

I followed in my rental truck as Floyd roared on ahead by ATV. We reached the spot and stopped, stepped out to walk, and as if by appointment it appeared on the horizon, glided straight in toward us like a strafing war plane, slowed, swooped up and hovered six feet overhead, and scolded with a gull-like cry: *B'yow! B'yow!* And then it landed on our heads, it really did: first Floyd's, then mine. But I was not content with this stunt alone, Floyd knew. We turned our eyes to the ground.

On his suggestion, we walked around each other in expanding circles, to see where we most elicited the bird's response—Floyd knew all about this game—and aptly it was he, Floyd, who found what we were looking for: a gray, dust-bunny youngster, plumped down on the tundra like a lump of lard. Which is in essence what it was: reconstituted lemming lard, with down, dark eyes, and the beak of a predator. Beside it lay a few odd scraps of vole or lemming, perhaps stowed for eating later.

It sat head up, regarding us with the indifference you'd expect of half a pound of lemming lard, but when I knelt to photograph it, the lard deigned to recognize me with a single bark: an imitation of its parent's cry, but weaker. I could not believe this bird's indifference to a beast two hundred times its size—or was it indolence? This baby jaeger had done little else but eat and sleep, after all, and watch the world go round about it: passing time as a living blob, in other words. Yet what a sleek and fleet-winged athlete it would one day be, as light and graceful in the air as anything that flies.

Was there a second young bird in the grass? There would have been, if only briefly; for the jaegers lay two eggs. But when food is scarce, the younger chick is the first to go without, and sorry to say, it quickly loses weight and dies.

Some years, Floyd says, there are no lemmings to be found at Barrow, and no jaegers. Some years all three can be found nesting on the tundra: Parasitic, Pomarine, and Long-tailed; but the Long-tailed is the scarcest. The local people know it from the others not by name, he says, but by its boldness. They know it as the one that will not only swoop in close and dive at you, and scold you, but land on your head.

LONG-TAILED JAEGER (ADULT) – BARROW, ALASKA, JULY 2012
Like their companions of the summer tundra, the Red and Red-necked Phalaropes, the jaegers spend most of their lives at sea. To them, the terra firma is a temporary need: fit only for their nesting.
"To watch the long-tailed jaeger in flight . . . with its long central tail feathers streaming in the wind," wrote Arthur Cleveland Bent, "is one of the delights of the Arctic summer."

WILSON'S PHALAROPES (YOUNG) – AUDUBON NWR, NORTH DAKOTA, JUNE 2012

VI

More Little Dears: The Shorebirds

FEW LIVING THINGS ON EARTH ARE AS ENDEARING AS THE YOUNG OF PLOVERS, SANDPIPERS, AND OTHER SHOREBIRDS, AND FEW ARE BLESSED WITH SUCH BOLD AND DEVOTED PARENTS.

Without the least consideration for its own fate, and no doubt a raging wish to flee, a parent bird will interpose itself between its young and a Godzilla predator of any size and drag itself away—pathetically, as if impaired by a near-lethal wound—until the beast is led so far astray it knows not where it started. The "ringed" (*Charadrius*) plovers are especially well known for their theatrical displays (pages 158–63), but others have their daring ploys as well: even the Least Sandpiper, the tiniest of the "peeps" (page 182).

In spite of such heroics, and the remarkably effective camouflage of the young birds themselves, predation takes a dreadful toll. Of a brood of four young plovers, say, the chances are that only one or two will live to feather out their wings and fly. But they don't know it, happily. They scoot about and pick at things, explore, find out about the world, and they do it earnestly—determinedly—as if it mattered. As if there were a life to live.

BLACK-NECKED STILT
Himantopus mexicanus

This stick-figure shorebird stilts its way about the shallows gracefully, and gently, but if its young are threatened it becomes an instant warrior, and its black needle bill a weapon. The birds pictured here became exactly that, a pair of warriors, when their chicks were threatened by a lone Great Egret gorging on young gallinules in a nearby clump of fire flag. As the poor gallinule parents stood by squawking, the egret seized and shook each young in turn, plunged it in water for a lubricating rinse, and gulped it down, head first—then snaked its neck into the fire flags for another.

It was no easy banquet for the egret, though. Not only were the gallinules squawking ever more desperately with every loss and flailing wings, even leaping at the villain, but a far more menacing attack was launched from overhead by the two Black-necked Stilts. While one bird of the pair stayed back to guard their own chicks, wings held up and over them like an umbrella, the other stilt was on the offensive: hovering, shrieking, swooping down and jabbing at the egret with its bill.

It wasn't clear that any jabs struck home, but the big egret croaked and lunged back in exasperation several times; so no, there was no peaceful picnicking for him in that found meal.

And in the meantime, while one stilt was still attacking from the air, his mate was shepherding their young away over the water. She folded up her long pink legs and swam, with all four young evacuees behind her.

Above:
(ADULT AND YOUNG) – PALM BEACH COUNTY, FLORIDA, JUNE 2010

Left:
(ADULT) – MATAGORDA ISLAND, TEXAS, APRIL 2009
The "deep-wading black-necked stilt," wrote naturalist Peter Matthiessen, "has the longest legs in proportion to its size than any bird on earth except the Greater Flamingo. . . ."

MORE LITTLE DEARS: THE SHOREBIRDS

Above:
BLACK-NECKED STILTS (YOUNG) – PALM BEACH COUNTY, FLORIDA, JUNE 2010
They're not yet two days old, but they're already swimming: to escape a rogue Great Egret on the prowl. A newborn stilt chick can not only swim, but dive—and then swim under water for as far as twenty feet.

Right:
BLACK-NECKED STILTS (ADULT AND YOUNG) – PALM BEACH COUNTY, FLORIDA, JUNE 2010

AMERICAN AVOCET
Recurvirostra americana

The phosphate lake at Chaplin, Saskatchewan, is an oasis crucial to sustaining the world's tundra-nesting shorebirds. Each spring, its soda-frosted flats and shores are host to migrants by the tens of thousands, including up to 50,000 Sanderlings (about half of the species' hemispheric population), all headed north to their arctic and sub-arctic breeding grounds. They stop to feed on the lake's billions of brine flies and brine shrimp, and refuel for the last long leg of their journey.

In the last days of June, with the passing of the northbound hordes, the wastes at Chaplin are abandoned by all but a handful of bird species. But among the handful are two nesting shorebirds that could not be more at home: the Piping Plover and the American Avocet. The avocet, especially: you could not invent a more inviting breeding ground for avocets.

Ask permission, drive the gravel road across in late June or July, and look to either side, and you can see the neat V's of young birds swimming out from shore. Their parents will have seen you coming and announced you when your car first showed on the horizon, and when you get there, they will be already airborne, calling out and overseeing the evacuation from above.

No call is more piercing and no doubt more irritating to a predator than the alarm call of the avocet, thanks in part to its uncanny simulation of the Doppler effect. As the bird flies in, it modulates its cries so that they rise increasingly in pitch, as if it were approaching even faster than it is.

And the evacuating chicks, meanwhile, are well equipped for an escape by water: they have big webbed feet, and down as waterproof as any duckling's.

Right:
(YOUNG) – CRANE LAKE, SASKATCHEWAN, JULY 2010

AMERICAN AVOCET (YOUNG) – CHAPLIN LAKE, SASKATCHEWAN, JULY 2010
At eye level, from a floating blind. So shallow was the sheet of water that the
photographer had to waddle in on his knees.

This shorebird works incessantly, frantically, and with the stamina of sand-pipers a fraction of its size; yet the effect is rhythmic, graceful, almost like dancing in the sky-blue water. It strides this way and that and swings the long neck to and fro, plunges the bill in to the hilt, and alternately sweeps the mud and stabs at it like a mad machine.

AMERICAN AVOCET (ADULT) – CRANE LAKE, SASKATCHEWAN, JULY 2007

(YOUNG) – BARROW, ALASKA, JULY 2012
"The voice of the dunlin, drifted down the tundras of the northern world from Greenland west to Somerset Island, and from Ireland eastward to Alaska, has been likened to the tinkling of ice in water." Peter Matthiessen, from *The Wind Birds.*

DUNLIN
Calidris alpina

In 1967, Peter Matthiessen opined that the Dunlin "may be the most numerous shorebird on earth." But would he say the same today? Slogging through its tundra breeding grounds at Churchill, Manitoba, on the shores of Hudson Bay, a person might think not.

Such was the impression of a visitor in July 2011, when much of this bird's prime nesting habitat was overgrazed by Canada Geese. The damage was dramatic: heads of sedges were cropped clean for acre upon acre, and the remaining blades so thin that you could see down to bare mud.

A nest shown to me by researchers was tucked into a foot-high hillock among grasses, mosses, creeping *ericads,* and sprinkled tundra flowers; and behind it, hunkered down and hiding, were four downy chicks: warm brown above with small white spots, and legs so long and gangly that it seemed their owners should have had a hard time standing upright. But stand they did, and *run.* When we intruders leaned down for a look, they scooted off through the surrounding sedges, over shallow pools and back around and up over the hillock, like exhilarated field mice.

The handsome hen stood on the hillock, calling in a rolling, bell-like trill, as if to orchestrate some kind of sensible response to the intrusion of two tall, untimely interlopers: one with a strapped-on shotgun (in case of a polar bear emergency) and one with a strapped-on camera.

Like any shorebird in the face of such intrusion, a good Dunlin parent might have intervened far more dramatically than that. One Dunlin with

a band of chicks, intruded on by Mr. Seton Gordon years ago in Scotland, "rushed up in alarm and literally rolled herself about on the ground with feath- ers ruffled."

DUNLIN (JUVENILE) – BARROW, ALASKA, JULY 2012

DUNLIN (JUVENILE) – BARROW, ALASKA, JULY 2012

Above:
DUNLIN (YOUNG) – CHURCHILL, MANITOBA, JULY 2011

Right:
DUNLIN (ADULT AND YOUNG) – CHURCHILL, MANITOBA, JULY 2012

Above:
(ADULT) – MATTAMUSKEET NWR, NORTH CAROLINA, MARCH 2011
In eight weeks, the ⅝-inch stub of the hatchling's bill will become the full 2½-inch "puddle-punching" instrument of the adult. Right:

Right:
(YOUNG) – TOWNER COUNTY, NORTH DAKOTA, JUNE 2011
So big are the legs and feet that they would seem to make up nearly half the bulk of the young bird.
For the first few days, a chick takes bits of food from the mud on its parents' bills: a rare case of dependency among the downy young of shorebirds, and one that earns the snipe the special designation "sub-precocial."

WILSON'S SNIPE
Gallinago delicata

Though said to be the most abundant shorebird in North America, the Wilson's Snipe is a shy tight-sitter, seldom seen unless it's nearly stepped on; and when flushed at last, it bursts away with a disdainful raspy *shhhaiyke,* as if dislodging it was the worst thing you could possibly have done. But it's the "winnowing" or "booming" of the snipe in spring for which this shorebird is, or ought to be, best known. Like the sportsman's famous timberdoodle, the woodcock, the snipe performs a courtship "flight song," which is really not a song at all, at least not in the conventional sense; it's a weird windy hooting made by the whoosh of air through the stiff feathers of its outer tail, and pulsating in concert with its wing beats. The winnow of the snipe is heard throughout the northern states and most of Canada, wherever there is boggy ground, and it's one of the most haunting sounds in all of nature.

Except for its distinctive bill, the streaked brown bird itself is a dull job indeed compared to the young chick, whose colors have to be the loveliest and most distinctive among all the downy shorebirds: a rich velvety mix of black, maroon, and chestnut, strewn with tiny puffs of white in cloud-like galaxies. And lovely though it is, the combination somehow serves as a remarkably effective camouflage.

It's a pity that this snipe chick has to be so brief a being, like all the other shorebird downies. In a week or so, it will become a grayed and frizzy in-between thing, and its beauty will be gone forever.

And in that week it will seclude itself among the moss and sedges of a bog, where almost certainly no human eyes will ever see it.

SHORT-BILLED DOWITCHER
Limnodromus griseus

Like the probing bills of woodcocks, snipe, and a few other shorebirds that depend upon small things that wriggle in deep mud, the Short-billed Dowitcher's is a two-part composite, and the part at the business end is a sophisticated instrument. It flexes independently, and is provided with small pits of touch receptor cells, called Herbst corpuscles, which can detect both pressure and vibration, and thus help the bird home in on those deep-lying worms and insect larvae and crustaceans.

Most shorebird chicks bear no resemblance to the adult birds from which they come, but this one does. The bill is a mere stub, foretelling nothing of the nearly three-inch instrument to come—it had to fit inside an inch-and-a-half-long eggshell, after all—but when you view the young and old birds standing side by side in profile, you can see at once: they are both dowitchers.

Throughout the early days of ornithology, the breeding grounds of the Short-billed Dowitcher remained a mystery. It was not until 1906 that the first nest and eggs were found, in northern Alberta, and for many years that nest was wrongly labeled "Long-billed Dowitcher."

Above:
(ADULT) – CHURCHILL, MANITOBA, JULY 2011

Left:
(YOUNG) – CHURCHILL, MANITOBA, JULY 2011
When the young birds hatch, only the male will likely be there with them. The female either has flown south already or soon will, and chances are that she will never see her progeny.

MORE LITTLE DEARS: THE SHOREBIRDS

AMERICAN GOLDEN-PLOVER
Pluvialis dominica

"I see *tigers*!" They were the startled words of Kat, my Manitoba bear guard, as she caught sight of two tiny fuzz balls in the grass.

Tigers: not the best of likenesses, of course. But then, to most of us the blacks and whites and swirling yellow golds of an American Golden-Plover chick present a sight so striking, so unlikely in the monotone of tundra green, that likenesses can only fail. They might as well be tiger stripes. Yet somehow, by some chromatic subterfuge, if you unfix your gaze for as much as a moment, those unlikely colors melt away—and they are not easy to relocate.

Among the other downy shorebirds, only one, the Wilson's Snipe, is both so lovely and so marvelously camouflaged.

The adult plovers linger with the young ones for a month or so, then fly off for the Southern Hemisphere, and three or four weeks after that the young ones—still only six or eight weeks old, with nothing but their inborn wits to guide them—embark on one of the most fantastic journeys made by any living thing. From Hudson Bay they fly southeast to the coast of Labrador, or south to New England, and then launch their nonstop 2,400-mile flight over the Atlantic Ocean to Brazil.

Only one bird on the planet migrates farther: the world champion Arctic Tern.

WATER BABIES

(ADULT) – CHURCHILL, MANITOBA, JULY 2011

(YOUNG) – CHURCHILL, MANITOBA, JULY 2011
*In six to ten weeks, this newly hatched chick will fly off for the
coast of Labrador, then southward over the Atlantic to Brazil.*

In Days Gone By

Two centuries ago, this shorebird was "even more numerous than the Eskimo Curlew, whose multitudes have been compared to the great flights of the passenger pigeon." So wrote Peter Matthiessen in 1967.*

In the early 1800s at Nantucket Island, Massachusetts, the ornithologist Edward Howe Forbush witnessed passing "waves" of both the plover and the curlew that "would almost darken the sun." At New Orleans two decades later, in 1821, John James Audubon witnessed a spring flock of "millions" of plovers, and estimated that 144,000 were shot.

But by the waning of the 19th Century, such sights would be no more. The American Golden-Plover would be so decimated at the hands of market gunners and sportsmen that, wrote Matthiessen, it "was fast following the Eskimo curlew toward oblivion."

Like the roving buffalo and Long-billed Curlew of the plains, the plover still holds on, but in a small sad fraction of its former numbers. Some shorebird species did come through the shooting orgy to recover a great portion of their former numbers, but not the golden-plover.

* *The Wind Birds.*

AMERICAN GOLDEN-PLOVER (ADULT) – BARROW, ALASKA, JULY 2012

SEMIPALMATED PLOVER
Charadrius semipalmatus

Dogs, foxes, weasels, even wily coyotes have been fooled by it.

It's called the broken wing act, and it's one of several tricks employed by a ground-nesting bird to save its eggs and young from the mouths of predators. A variety of birds rely on it, but most famously the shorebirds, and most famously of all the "ringed" (*Charadrius*) plovers: the common Killdeer, notably, but also its close relative, the Semipalmated Plover.

The plover pictured here put on a sequence of displays for me, and held each one in pause for many seconds, as if before a row of judges: tail spread open, flagrantly; one wing and then the other wing held up, then down; both wings held out straight like an airplane's; and head pressed flat to the ground with the jaw frozen open, as if the bird were paralyzed.

In its nest among the rocks and lichens, meanwhile, lay the beneficiary of all these theatrics: a single chick, wet and bedraggled, and a most pathetic bit of bird. Was it alive? The down was stuck fast to its skin in places, and in places absent altogether, and the rest of it seemed stitched in bundles, as if it were no living bird at all, but a bedraggled old toy mouse left by a house cat.

I almost pitied the poor thing that it should have to be alive. And yet few chicks of any kind are so quick to come to life, and do it with such vigor, as a Semipalmated Plover. Within hours this bit among the rubble would be standing on a pair of long, strong legs, and at the slightest provocation would be off and running.

And man, can that young bird *run*.

Above:
(YOUNG) – CHURCHILL, MANITOBA, JULY 2011
It stops for a half second. . . . Runs. Stops for a half second. . . . Runs. And when it runs, it runs like crazy. The tot in the photo was the very devil to get the lens focused up on.

Left:
(ADULT) – CHURCHILL, MANITOBA, JULY 2011
Near its nest, on the stony shores of Hudson Bay: it's trying to distract you.

(YOUNG) – OLD LYME, CONNECTICUT, MAY 2013
*Like the Semipalmated, this two-inch plover chick can run like
crazy. It took the photographer enormous effort, and much
luck, to catch this millisecond instant.*

PIPING PLOVER
Charadrius melodus

The Piping Plover chick, like the adult—and like other shorebird chicks—is a marvel of protective coloration. Unless it moves, and sometimes even when it does, you'll have a hard time seeing it: even if it's only steps away, and pointed out to you; and even if it's peeping. Even the young bird's peeping is ventriloquial.

The old New England bird man Edward Howe Forbush, not a dim observer, once picked up a downy plover from the beach and then released it. "It ran a little way," he wrote, "and I have never seen it since. The most careful search failed to solve this puzzle."

He was not the only man to be so puzzled. What most impresses me about the downy youngster, though, is its precocity, and in particular how soon a newly hatched chick can run—and fast. So I'm a little puzzled by Forbush's later capture of "four lively youngsters" less than a day old. "They were so active," wrote Mr. Forbush, "that if one were liberated it would be rather difficult to catch it."

Rather difficult to catch it? I've happened on these two-inch tots myself a few times, and seen them run, and I can only say that I'm in awe of what could have only been the man's capacity for understatement.

I'd wanted for the longest time to photograph one running, and I'd tried—in fact I tried with one bird many, many times, over the course of several days—and I tell you that this motor-powered chick could *run*. It streaked across a muddy flat in bursts, head down, legs buzzing in a yellow blur . . . though really I should not have said *across* the muddy flat, but *over* it; for this white little ball

appeared to travel through a medium of air alone, suspended by the whir of its propeller legs. As far as I could see, no yellow touched the mud.

And when I got my photograph, at last—not of a blurred white head or fleeting rump alone, or mud alone, but the whole downy ball—it seemed that my impression wasn't so far off.

It runs like it's flying.

(ADULT) – OLD LYME, CONNECTICUT, MAY 2013
The call is the enchanting thing: the mellow "piping" has a wistful, almost melancholy quality, and it's ventriloquial, too. The old-time bird man Winsor Tyler wrote of it as "a soft musical moan, we can not tell from where. . . ."

PIPING PLOVER (YOUNG) – OLD LYME, CONNECTICUT, MAY 2013

PIPING PLOVER (ADULT) – OLD LYME, CONNECTICUT, MAY 2013

Above and right:
(YOUNG) – BARROW, ALASKA, JULY 2012
First swimming, in a tundra pool. In six more weeks this same bird will be bobbing on the oceans of another hemisphere, and will not see land again until it returns north in spring.

RED-NECKED PHALAROPE
Phalaropus lobatus

It's the iconoclastic way of all the phalaropes that she, not he, displays the brighter colors; and that once she lays the eggs, her work is done. She leaves the rest—the incubation of the eggs, the tending of the young—to him.

It's their way that they should swim, too. The down on their bellies is as ample as a duckling's, and they bob on the water as buoyant as corks. They are a family of contrarians, these phalaropes; they break the rules. They are the sandpipers that swim.

The downy chicks swim, too. No sooner are they hatched out and dried off than the male marches them down the nesting hummock and off to the nearest pool, where they will find not only a lush insect life to feed upon, but a lush growth of sedges to conceal them from the eyes of predators.

Stand watch beside a tundra pool at Churchill, Manitoba, in the first weeks of July, and you might see one of these downy puffballs sally out from shore while its male parent watches from a few yards back: its own on-duty lifeguard. It seems a premature and foolhardy adventure, for the chick is plainly striving, bobbed by the ripples and skewed by the slightest breezes; but he perseveres.

Talk about *precocial*. In about five weeks, the first small bands of fledgling phalaropes will fly away southeast over tundra, muskeg, and boreal forest to the rocky shores of the Atlantic, and then off to the rolling oceans of the Southern Hemisphere—off Africa, perhaps, or South America—where they while away the winter feeding on zooplankton. And they will do all that without the help of any compass, map, or grown-up bird to guide them.

Their parents will have left already, weeks before.

Above:
RED-NECKED PHALAROPE (ADULT) – CHURCHILL, MANITOBA, JULY 2011

Right:
RED-NECKED PHALAROPE (YOUNG) – CHURCHILL, MANITOBA, JULY 2011
A downy chick, just hatched, emerges from its natal clump of tundra.

RED PHALAROPE
Phalaropus fulicarius

You first hear their calls, sharp *peet*s among the rough *k-chuck* notes of the Red-neckeds, as mixed flocks of the two phalaropes fly in across the tundra, veer off toward one likely pool and then another, swoop in suddenly as if to land and then swoop up, then down again, and splash feet-first into another. And no sooner have they folded up their wings than they are busy working, swimming, bills pointed down and picking as they go. Then they are up and off again, veering and *peet*ing and splash-landing in another pool.

On the tundra east of Barrow, the blue summer pools are never long without a pair or two of this most northern and most striking of the phalaropes, and I could no more miss their brick reds on the water than their *peet* calls overhead. But they were growing fewer, almost by the hour. Along the road I often heard among the *peet*s a dreadful *twang*, and looked up to the power lines to see a body stopped short in the air and parachuting down.

The fuzzy young ones, though, were nowhere to be seen. They were out there, in the wet depressions, never far from the on-duty males but always deep among the sedges and the reddish *Arctophila* grass, and screened from view. Like the chicks of Red-necked Phalaropes, they are no sooner hatched and standing up than they are led off to the marshy pools, where they thrive in safety on a never-ending fund of insects.

(YOUNG) – BARROW, ALASKA, JULY 2012

RED PHALAROPE (ADULT) – BARROW, ALASKA, JULY 2012
This least-known and least accessible of the phalaropes spends up to eleven months a year at sea. It returns to the tundra's terra "firma" only to nest.

RED PHALAROPE (YOUNG) – BARROW, ALASKA, JULY 2012

WILSON'S PHALAROPE
Phalaropus tricolor

It swims as well as any phalarope, and heeds the rule of reversed gender roles. But in some respects, the Wilson's is the non-conformist in a family of non-conformists.

It nests not on the arctic tundra with the other two but on the Northern Plains, where it consorts with the American Avocet. Unlike the Red and Red-necked Phalaropes, both circumpolar nesting birds, the Wilson's is confined exclusively to the Americas: to North America in summer, and in winter South America, where it repairs to the high-elevation lakes of the central Andes. It's the American phalarope.

And when it departs in fall it doesn't flee land altogether for the open oceans, like the others; it keeps to the shores and coastal marshes, where it keeps company with ordinary peeps and yellowlegs.

Even as a nestling, from the moment it first pecks and pries its way free of the eggshell, the Wilson's is a different kind of phalarope. Its down is golden buff throughout, with irregular black markings on the upperparts: a design not only beautiful, but unlike that of any other downy shorebird. And though it swims as well as any downy phalarope, it's not possessed by the aquatic mania that drives the other two. Unlike those lunatics, the Wilson's isn't hell-bent on the march to water from the moment it can first stand up and walk.

It takes its time, and ambles out over the grassland for a mile or more, if need be, before it gets its feet wet.

173

Above:
(ADULT) – CRANE LAKE, SASKATCHEWAN, JULY 2007

Left:
(YOUNG) – AUDUBON NWR, NORTH DAKOTA, JUNE 2012
Seen at that rarest and most critical of life moments: newly hatched, dried off, and stepping out into the Great Unknown. They will not come back.

WHIMBREL
Numenius phaeopus

Hudsonian Curlew: could any other bird name so evoke the romance of the distant wild? That was its common name not many years ago, and what a pity that it is no longer.

As a teenager, I had despaired of ever seeing this grand shorebird with the "sickle bill," but then one August morning in Connecticut, in the fields down by the shore—I was fifteen—it happened. The great bird rose up from the grass with a wild piercing cry, big as a duck and golden brown, magnificent with its long, curved bill, then flew out over the waters of Long Island Sound, turned west, and winged down the coast until it disappeared.

I could hardly believe I'd really seen it: the Hudsonian Curlew.

On the western shores of Hudson Bay, the Whimbrel nests on vast sedge meadows broken only by shallow pools and spindly tamaracks; and on one such meadow fifty-plus years later, more than a mile out from the lone dirt road, researcher Hannah Specht showed me the nest where a single chick had hatched. He had somehow got himself upended and was lying on his back, feet pawing at the air in what seemed a half-hearted effort to get righted, so we backed off to wait and let the proper party do the righting: the parent.

You'd never know it was a Whimbrel. Apart from his big feet and his amusing upside-down act—which he seemed to enjoy, like a human baby on his back, amused by passing clouds—what seemed so remarkable about this baby was his bill: it was so *un*remarkable. But that's how it is with the chicks of curlews, godwits, and other shorebirds destined to inherit the long fancy bills: for the first two weeks, those bills are short and straight and altogether

unremarkable. They have to be, of course. They have to fit inside a 2¼-inch-long eggshell, and a chick needs to be in there, too.

But still, that Whimbrel chick was a surprise. I thought it would betray at least a hint of the great sickle bill to come.

(ADULT AND YOUNG) – CHURCHILL, MANITOBA, JULY 2011

Above:
WIMBREL (ADULT) – CHURCHILL, MANITOBA, JULY 2011

Right:
WIMBREL (YOUNG) – CHURCHILL, MANITOBA, JULY 2011
A newly hatched chick: bottomside up, but in no hurry to correct the situation.
The ⅝-inch bill is just a fifth of its full future length of more than 3 inches, and
will show no sign of the "sickle" curve for at least twelve days.

PECTORAL SANDPIPER
Calidris melanotos

The old-time market gunners knew it as the "grass snipe," and aptly so, for even on migration Pectorals seek out grassy habitats—wet meadows, short-grass marshes—that most suggest their breeding grounds far to the north.

Around the town of Barrow, Alaska, the Pectoral is not only the most common breeding shorebird, but possibly the most abundant breeding bird of any kind (except in higher, drier habitats, where it's outnumbered by the Lapland Longspur). You find it nesting almost anywhere you find wet tundra, and that's almost everywhere.

By the middle of July, every female Pectoral you see will mark the presence of four chicks you don't see. They are nearby, within a few yards of their guardian, and while it may be tempting to march straight in to catch a glimpse, you'd only be wasting your time. Before you've even closed the car door, she will announce you, and the chicks will tuck in deep among the stems and freeze, so well concealed that you would have to scrutinize each step with agonizing care. And only after you are gone—or you pretend to be gone, while sitting in your vehicle—only then will she sound the all-clear and the chicks come back to life, emerge, and reply with peeping notes that only she can locate.

The safe, sure way to see the chicks of any shorebird on the tundra is to keep watch through the window of your "rolling blind": parked on the roadside, with the engine off.

Above:
(ADULT) – BARROW, ALASKA, JULY 2012

Left:
(YOUNG) – BARROW, ALASKA, JULY 2012

Above left:
PECTORAL SANDPIPER (YOUNG) – BARROW, ALASKA, JULY 2012

Above right:
DUNLIN (YOUNG) – BARROW, ALASKA, JULY 2012

Which Is Which?

Two sandpipers, one a Dunlin and one a Pectoral—but which is which?

As adults, the two could hardly look more different; but the chicks could not be more alike.

The rich brown upperparts; the fine white spotting; the dark bills; the fancy face patterns, right down to the two broken "mustache" lines . . . in every case, the details are the same for both of these young sandpipers. To study them for differences is asking for a headache.

But again the adults are so different, not only in coloration and morphology (compare the bills!) but in their chosen habitat, winter range. . . . So how can the chicks be such close copies of each other?

Biologically, in fact, the two are not so different. Like the Least, Semipalmated, and other small "peep" sandpipers, the Pectoral (*left*) and the Dunlin (*right*) belong to the same genus: they are both *Calidris* sandpipers.

Close relatives, in other words. Unlikely ones—but close.

You can't help thinking that there must be some way to distinguish them, though; and there is. On close inspection, you will see that while the Dunlin's bill is dark slaty gray throughout, the Pectoral's lightens at the base to a pale brown. And while the Dunlin's brownish legs and feet have a distinct *reddish* cast, the Pectoral's have no such cast.

Above:
(ADULT) – CHURCHILL, MANITOBA, JULY 2011
The full-grown bird weighs 25 to 30 grams—one ounce—but there's nothing "least" about this sandpiper's determination when its nest or young are threatened. It stands fast before a predator of any size and turns its back, spreads wide its tail, and agitates its wings, all to divert attention from what matters most: its four brown chicks.

Right:
(YOUNG) – CHURCHILL, MANITOBA, JULY 2011
The rich brown upperparts of this and certain other downy sandpipers—the Pectoral, for instance, and the two dowitchers, and Wilson's Snipe—are broken up by bold black lines and bars and spots, and tiny puffs of white (or buffy white). The whitish puffs are formed by rigid tips of down, called "bottle brush" feathers, bound tight by tiny barbules; and pretty though they are, they have a purpose: to help hide the bird. Could they not pass for the small fruiting bodies of a moss?

LEAST SANDPIPER
Calidris minutilla

The Least is the smallest of the "peeps"—five small sparrow-like sandpipers so vexingly alike that a birdwatching newcomer might think them hardly worth the bother—but it is so common, and so easy to identify, that it's the ideal species of comparison: the touchstone peep. Its size, its mud-brown upperparts and predilection for muddy shores, and its bright yellow legs and feet all combine to make it the peep made-to-order for beginners.

At four grams each, the newly hatched chicks are truly minuscule, but within hours of hatching they are off in search of wetter, richer pastures, never to return. And they are *quick*. When you approach, they dart away among the sedges like excited mice, this way and that, with such celerity that the eye, not to say the clumsy camera, can hardly follow.

And like other shorebird chicks, they are marvelously camouflaged. The rich brown back is sprinkled with white spots that tend to cluster in the shape of an hourglass or an angled cross—and which bear an uncanny likeness to the tundra mosses at your feet.

Crouched among the sedges, mud, and moss, this chick no more attracts your eye than any other two square inches of the tundra.

LEAST BITTERNS (YOUNG) – SQUAW CREEK NWR, MISSOURI, JUNE 1994

VII

More Comic Monsters: The Bitterns

THE BITTERNS ARE HERONS, TECHNICALLY—THEY BELONG TO THE FAMILY *ARDEIDAE*— BUT UNLIKE THEIR MORE ORNAMENTAL RELATIVES, THEY ARE BUILT LESS TO BE ADMIRED THAN OVERLOOKED.

Seen close up, they are a little goofy looking, with bottom-heavy bellies and elastic necks, and eyes set low upon the head: to see what's going on below, presumably, while the rest of the bird points upward to the sky. This is the famous bittern trick, called "bitterning": to stretch straight up and freeze, and mimic the surrounding reeds.

So artful is their mimicry that if a breeze comes up, and the reeds sway, the bittern will sway slowly with them.

The nests of bitterns are among the marsh's best-kept secrets, and a far cry from the elevated tree nests of most other herons. And they are not massed together but placed singly, though in some southern states Least Bitterns sometimes congregate in loosely scattered "colonies."

What strikes you first about the nestlings is how vertical they are, and how *uniformly* vertical. They stand as one, whether as still as the surrounding reeds (Least Bittern) or reared up and snapping, pretending to be seasoned tough guys (American); and they are a sight you will remember, either way.

It's a treat to see a bittern, always. And to see a *baby* bittern—that's a treat far greater still.

AMERICAN BITTERN
Botaurus lentiginosus

Unlike the Least Bittern, ever clambering and seeking, the American Bittern prefers to sit and wait and take what comes its way. It stands immobile, hunched or leaning like a crooked stake, a harmless sight to the unwary frog or fish or tadpole, snake, or anything else that happens by too close and is not too big to swallow; but then lightning quick it comes alive—and strikes.

The most curious thing about the bittern is the deep, pneumatic call it sends across the marsh in spring, often under the cover of dusk or darkness: without a doubt, one of the wildest, weirdest sounds in all of nature. When a bittern calls, you do not really hear it, at first; you sense it. You feel its basso presence as you would a distant thunder rumble.

The call sounds like a pump, or at a distance like the smacking of a stake into soggy ground. Indeed, its call has earned the bittern a rich list of nicknames: plum-pudd'n, thunder-pumper, stake driver, pump-er-lunk, dunk-a-doo, barrel-maker, bog bull, butterpump, mire drum, water belcher. Actually, the "voice" of the bittern is a well-modulated belching, produced by the expulsion of great gulps of air.

While young Least Bitterns point up their bills and freeze when you approach, the more robust young of this bittern will rear up and clack their bills at you and hiss, but with some hesitation, as if they were conflicted: should they be unseen or seen, inanimate or live? Fixed as the cattail blades, or fiery-eyed defenders? They can't quite fulfill either role, it appears. Not yet.

Above:
(ADULT) – STUTSMAN COUNTY, NORTH DAKOTA, JUNE 1994

Left:
(YOUNG) – STUTSMAN COUNTY, NORTH DAKOTA, JUNE 1994

A Baby Bittern Plays *Nursemaid*?

Half a century ago in Manitoba, the ornithologist Margaret Morse Nice kept watch on a newly hatched bittern in captivity, and observed that it began to lunge at objects when it was just 80 minutes old.

When four days old, it was placed with a brood of newly hatched Soras, and its first move was to lunge at one and try to swallow it. Thereafter it remained not only peaceable but "very patient" with its younger charges, allowing them to cuddle under it and even pester it for food.

Only when a Sora tried to nestle under it again the next day did the bittern finally take a nip at it.

Beware of that dagger bill, for heaven's sake, if you should ever have a close encounter with a bittern. Keep your face away—your eyes, especially—for these birds can strike as lightning-quick as any of the herons. Roger Tory Peterson once caught an injured American Bittern, which expressed its displeasure with a strike straight for his eyes. Peterson's reflexes were also quick, however, and he jerked his head away, but not before the bittern struck him just above the upper lip, leaving a small scar.

"Because of that bittern," he later jested, "I could never grow a mustache."

AMERICAN BITTERN (ADULT) – STUTSMAN COUNTY,
NORTH DAKOTA, JUNE 1994

LEAST BITTERN
Ixobrychus exilis

This smallest of the herons is a true shape-shifter, able to compress itself and glide through the slim spaces of a marsh with ease. John James Audubon once kept a pet Least Bittern, and observed that though the bird was at least two inches wide, it could slip through two bookends spaced an inch apart. In some ways, this heron is more like the rails than its own kind.

Unlike the bulkier American Bittern, it clambers through the upper story of the marsh and straddles, juts out horizontally, even clings and hangs with bottom up and bill aimed down: it may try anything. But when alarmed, it draws itself into a figure slim and upright as the reeds, and melts away—all but the yellow eyes.

When discovered at their nest, the young respond in perfect synchrony, and instantly, as if all wired to the same switch. Part the cattails and peer in, and you'll see every bittern neck stretched upward, every bill inclined at the same angle—and that's how they will remain, rock-solid as if cast in bronze. Not one head is turned askew, not one bill out of parallel.

There are no mavericks among Least Bittern chicks.

Above:
(YOUNG) – SQUAW CREEK NWR, MISSOURI, JUNE 1994

Right:
(ADULT) – SQUAW CREEK NWR, MISSOURI, JUNE 1994

WATER BABIES

Above:
LEAST BITTERN (YOUNG) – POLK COUNTY, IOWA, JUNE 1994

Right:
LEAST BITTERN (ADULT) – OLD LYME, CONNECTICUT, AUGUST 1994

WILSON'S SNIPE (ADULT) – STUTSMAN COUNTY, NORTH DAKOTA, JUNE 2013

PHOTOGRAPHING *WATER BABIES*

Most downy chicks are smaller, quicker, better camouflaged, and more adroit at hiding than adults, so they can be a bit more challenging; but by and large it takes the same equipment, tactics, and techniques to photograph them. Nonetheless, insofar as my approaches differ from the norm at times, some readers may be interested to know them in detail: so here they are.

Described below are the three fundamental means by which I made these *Water Babies* photos, of young birds and old alike:

I. "PORTABLE STUDIO" FLASH OUTFIT

I designed this outfit years ago to photograph two mousy rails of the night marsh. It incorporates two major flash units, main and fill, with diffusion screens and camera, power winder, macro lens (100mm or 200mm), and a light to see and focus by, all mounted to an aluminum frame with struts and an extending shoulder brace: so it's a bit unwieldy, and not always easy to explain to passersby, but it's effective. Though portable, it produced a powerful but soft, studio-quality light you couldn't tell from daylight, and you could count on it to do so anytime and anywhere: even in the middle of a salt marsh, in the middle of the night.

There was one hitch to this "portable studio" approach, however. You had to get in close—within three to six feet of the bird, eight feet at most—and not all birds will let you do that.

The photographs of Least and American Bitterns were made with this all-flash arrangement, from as close as three to four feet.

II. ROVING FREE WITH HAND-HELD CAMERA

When you can't get that close, and when the subject isn't apt to be as stationary as a bittern—and when hauling cumbersome equipment is impossible or undesirable (as it often is for me these days)—this is the way to go: no blind, no tripod, no gear at all to tie you down except for a single camera, lens, and camera-mounted flash. I'm simply prowling on my own, whether in search of one bird in particular or ranging free: for "targets of opportunity," as the old fighter pilots used to say. When I'm in this roving mode, my lens is usually the popular 100-400mm zoom; when working closer than its minimum focus distance of about six feet, of course, I use a shorter lens.

Most of the shorebirds here, and many others, were photographed in this easygoing footloose way.

III. THE FLOATING BLIND

A *floating* blind, indeed: to photograph the water birds of prairie lakes and ponds, young and adult, it was essential. I designed the thing so that it broke down into modular components that could fit inside a car: three foam pontoons and an unfolding aluminum frame; a "cowcatcher" in front to fend off floating reeds and other flotsam; and a portholed fabric cover to conceal the man within. Other features included hooks and tie lines, an adjusting camera post, flash mounts, and snap-on storage boxes. I should add that this contraption was designed for use in relatively shallow, solid-bottomed prairie lakes, and not in water more than chest deep (that was the intent, at least); and that the craft alone was meant to do the floating, never the photographer. He merely did the pushing, and the piloting.

There's nothing quite like moving out among the wild birds of the water at their own eye level with your lens and camera mounted at the ready, and then framing up your subject while he goes about his business, blithely, as if you were no more unwelcome than another coot or clump of reeds. For all the inconvenience, few moments are more thrilling.

But I've had a few uneasy moments in that floating blind, as well: like when I looked out the back one afternoon to see the jet-black wall of an approaching storm, and lightning flashing.

Most photographs were taken by the second means described above—with a hand-held camera, prowling—and with the use of fill flash. But had it not been for two recent innovations, in most cases they could not have been: "Image Stabilization," which mitigates the effects of camera shake (and motion blur) by as much as three to four full f-stops; and, more crucial still, the "High Speed Flash Sync" feature now available with camera makers' dedicated flash units.

Virtually every one of these *Water Babies* subjects, even those in the soft natural light of overcast or shade, received at least a touch of fill flash: if only to add catchlights to the eyes or enhance the texture of dull feather edgings. And not so many years ago, you couldn't do that: not with the shutter speeds required to stop the motion of a living bird. Before the late 1990s, your flash couldn't synchronize with focal plane shutter speeds beyond 1/250 second.

When working at a subject distance of ten feet or more, I often used one of those funky flash extenders (called a "beamer"), which is little more than a cast-plastic fresnel lens held six inches from the flash head by two molded plastic arms, which are in turn retained by strips of Velcro. It's cheesy looking, but effective.

The advent of these two essential innovations—Image Stabilization and, especially, High Speed Flash Sync—has been a boon to all hand-held photography. Without them, and without the earlier introduction of auto-focus lenses, hand-held photography of birds in motion would still be a game of hit-and-miss, and mostly miss.

Just five years ago, after 35 years of allegiance to the Kodachromes—last man to leave the gate?—I made the switch. Most photos you see here were made with a 'D' camera (Canon EOS 40D and [primarily] 7D), and three lenses (also Canon): EF 500mm f4, EF 100-400mm f4.5-5.6 zoom, and EF 28-135mm f3.5-5.6 zoom. I use Canon 580-EX II flash units.

The few photographs made with the "portable studio" flash outfit described above were made with a Canon F-1 film camera and three Canon FD macro lenses: 50mm (rarely), 100mm, and 200mm.

None of these photos are of captive birds, or of birds baited in any way. No props or perches were placed in the pictures, nor has anything been materially added or enhanced by means of Photoshop or other image programs. All scenes are exactly as they occurred in nature, except that at the nest of an American Bittern the foreground grass was held back temporarily and then brushed back into place.

FURTHER READING

Books on birds—on adult birds, that is to say—are many, and need no further mention here. But if you wish to learn about the same birds in their early incarnations, as downy young, your books are few.

Those titles I've found both illuminating and engaging fall into these fundamental categories: **general "field guide,"** **"literary scientific"** (oxymoronic though it sounds), **breeding birds by region** (for example, of North Dakota, or of the arctic), **breeding birds by family group** (for example, shorebirds, or waterfowl), and **life histories** (the two series are veritable libraries in themselves, yet different as two works could be).

GENERAL "FIELD GUIDE"

Baicich, Paul, and Colin Harrison. 1997. *A Guide to the Nests, Eggs and Nestlings of North American Birds.* London: Academic Press.

A useful, indeed virtually the only, general guide to downy young birds of North America. Includes synopses of nesting natural history, compiled from other sources. Many species nicely illustrated with paintings, but by no means all: not a complete guide.

"LITERARY SCIENTIFIC"

Matthiessen, Peter. 1967. *The Wind Birds.* New York: Viking Press.

If you read only one book about shorebirds—indeed, if you read only one book about birds—read Peter Matthies-

sen's *The Wind Birds.* A lyrical, exacting, intelligent portrait of this affecting group.

Nice, Margaret Morse. 1962. *Development of Behavior in Precocial Birds.* Transactions of the Linnaean Society 3. New York: Linnaean Society of New York.

A singularly readable, insightful, often compelling inquiry into the early lives of waterfowl and other precocial birds.

BREEDING BIRDS BY REGION

EASTERN U.S.

Forbush, E. H. 1927. *Birds of Massachusetts and Other New England States.* Boston: Commonwealth of Massachusetts.

Antiquated, but with lively observations of the downy young of some species (for example, Piping Plover, Black-crowned Night Heron).

Stone, Witmer. 1937. *Bird Studies at Old Cape May.* Philadelphia: Academy of Natural Sciences (reprint 1965; New York: Dover).

Like Forbush's work, above, but on those birds nesting one step farther south.

NORTHERN PLAINS, PRAIRIES, AND THE MIDDLE WEST

Chapman, Frank M. 1908. *Camps and Cruises of an Ornithologist.* New York: D. Appleton and Co.

Writing is somewhat stiff, antiquated; but includes

absorbing chapters on the author's travels to the plains and prairies for nesting birds. Accompanied by black and white photos.

Job, Herbert K. 1902. *Among the Waterfowl.* New York: Doubleday, Page & Co.

Personal accounts of an old-timer in search of nesting water birds in North Dakota and elsewhere. Accompanied by evocative black and white photos.

Stewart, Robert E. 1975. *Breeding Birds of North Dakota.* Fargo: Tri-College Center for Environmental Studies.

The last word on the breeding birds of this key northern prairie state.

ARCTIC TUNDRA

Jehl, Joseph R. Jr., and Blanche A. Smith. 1970. *Birds of the Churchill Region, Manitoba.* Winnipeg: Manitoba Museum of Man and Nature.

The book on the breeding birds of the western shores of Hudson Bay.

Vaughn, Richard. 1992. *In Search of Arctic Birds.* London: T & AD Poyser.

An inspired survey of birds on their arctic breeding grounds, enriched with place descriptions and historical accounts. Accompanied by black and white photos.

BREEDING BIRDS BY FAMILY GROUP

SHOREBIRDS

Matthiessen, Peter. 1967. *The Wind Birds.* New York: Viking Press.

If you read only one book about shorebirds—indeed, if you read only one book about birds—read Peter Matthiessen's *The Wind Birds.* A lyrical, exacting, intelligent portrait of this affecting group.

Tuck, Leslie M. 1972. *The Snipes: A Study of the Genus Capella.* Canadian Wildlife Monograph Series 5. Ottawa: Canadian Wildlife Service.

That's right, a book on snipes alone—and it's a comprehensive one, if you want a resource on the Wilson's Snipe.

HERONS, WADING BIRDS

Hancock, James A. 2000. *Herons of North America: Their World in Focus.* London: Academic Press.

Color photos generally unsophisticated and uninspired, but otherwise a worthwhile introduction to North America's breeding herons, with information on each species' nesting life.

SEABIRDS

Fisher, James, and R. M. Lockley. 1954. *Sea-Birds: An Introduction.* Boston: Houghton Mifflin.

Informative; by two Brits who knew their seabirds.

Gaston, Anthony J. 2004. *Seabirds: A Natural History.* New Haven: Yale University Press.

Also informative, but newer; by a Canadian who knows his seabirds.

WATERFOWL

Kortright, Francis H., and T. M. Shortt. 1942. *Ducks, Geese, and Swans of North America.* Washington, DC: American Wildlife Institute.

This popular and most comprehensive work has appeared in several incarnations—most recently the two-volume slipcased edition by Guy M. Bladassare, published by Johns Hopkins University Press in 2014.

Nelson, Colleen Helgeson. 1995. *The Downy Waterfowl of North America.* Deerfield, Illinois: Delta Station Press.

A thorough, detailed, and scholarly work, richly illustrated by the author's paintings. Not a practical guide to duckling identification.

LIFE HISTORIES

The ultimate resources. There are two series, two vast repositories of information on all aspects of North American bird biographies (voice, behavior, habitat and range, migration routes, nests and eggs, young, etc.). The two could hardly be more different: one is the more modern resource, and one a joy to read.

For the more up-to-date and (usually) reliably accurate accounts, the obvious choice is the current *Birds of North America* series, the print version of which was completed in 2002 and published jointly by The American Ornithologists' Union and The Academy of Natural Sciences of Philadelphia. The entire work is now available online as a project of the Cornell Lab of Ornithology. If you're an academic ornithologist, this is your source. Access is by paid subscription.

For atmosphere and personality, a sense of place and history, and the immediacy of firsthand accounts—for "life" and "history" in their fullest senses, you might say—the choice is just as obvious: the 26 volumes of Arthur Cleveland Bent's timeless *Life Histories of North American Birds*, published by the Smithsonian between 1919 (diving birds) and 1968 (sparrows, etc.). All volumes were superbly reprinted in Dover paperback editions, and all are available online for free from the Biodiversity Heritage Library.

If you had no other books on birds but Bent's *Life Histories*, you'd have a mighty library. They are incomparable.

Two other titles might be mentioned for their fine-art paintings of young birds—subjects not often portrayed in that medium, to say the least:

Johnsgard, Paul A. 1998 (repr. 2006). *Baby Bird Portraits by George Miksch Sutton: Watercolors in the Field Museum*. Norman: University of Oklahoma Press.

Most of Sutton's 19 subjects are altricial species (for example, Horned Lark, Henslow's Sparrow), but two are precocial birds of the wetlands: Common Gallinule and White-rumped Sandpiper. The White-rumped is a beauty.

Marcham, Frederick George, ed. 1971. *Louis Agassiz Fuertes and the Singular Beauty of Birds*. New York: HarperCollins.

A collection of the artist's letters and paintings, with foreword by Dean Amadon and introduction by Roger Tory Peterson. Only two precocial downies are included (Horned Grebe, Black-necked Stilt), but they are beauties.

BLACK-NECKED STILTS (ADULT AND YOUNG) – PALM BEACH COUNTY, FLORIDA, JUNE 2010

ACKNOWLEDGMENTS

Without the help of those biologists and naturalists acquainted with the breeding birds of their home regions—and I mean both their direct help in the field and their help in pointing me to productive destinations—not only would this effort have been less enjoyable, but I'd have made only a fraction of the photographs you see.

So first of all I'm grateful to the following:

Saskatchewan: Brian Hepworth, of Ducks Unlimited, Regina; Brad Vilness, of Sidewood; C. Stuart Houston, of Saskatoon, for introducing me to the Churchill Northern Studies Center; and special thanks to Clem Millar, Chairman of the Chaplin Nature Center (among other things), for acquainting a foreigner with the perils of Chaplin Lake so that he wouldn't stray and disappear in phosphate quicksand.

North Dakota: Thanks to my friends at Northern Prairie Research Center in Jamestown: Doug Johnson (again you've been so very helpful, Doug), Ray Greenwood (*again* thanks for the bitterns), Marsha Sovada, and Larry Igl; and thanks again Dave Lambeth of Grand Forks for putting me in touch with Northern Prairie in the first place, all those years ago.

Particular thanks of late to Neal Niemuth, of the USFWS at Bismarck; Frank Rohwer, of Delta Waterfowl, for his considerable help during several stays in Towner County; Jim Fisher, also of Delta Waterfowl; Jim Ringleman, of Ducks Unlimited; Paulette Scherr, at Arrowwood NWR; Mark Fisher, USFWS at Devils Lake; and Lloyd Jones, Refuge Manager (ret.) at Audubon NWR. For recent help in steering me toward Western Grebes, thanks to Rick Bohn; Eric Weber; Ron Martin; and thanks to Mrs. Richard Sabinash for her kind permission to photograph on private land.

I'm enormously grateful to Jackie Jacobson, Visitor Services Manager at Audubon NWR: thanks for those two days and your keen eye, Jackie—and those funky night herons.

Maryland: Harry (Henry T.) Armistead; Bill Hubick; Matt Perry; Paul Spitzer; and thanks especially to Dave Hoffman, and to Peter McGowan of the USFWS.

Florida: Jim Shadle; Arthur Morris; and especially Nancy Elwood.

Louisiana: Charles Bush.

Churchill, Manitoba: Thanks to the people at the Churchill Northern Studies Centre, for help and accommodation in July 2011: in particular LeeAnn Fishback, Scientific Coordinator, and "bear guides" Katrina Jansen and Carley Basler; and above all thanks to those Churchill shorebird researchers of 2011, who without exception went out of their way to steer me toward my subjects: Andy Johnson;

Laura McKinnon; Carmen Lishman (thanks Carmen for those dowitchers); Nathan Senner; Anne Corkery; and Hannah Specht (thank you, Hannah, for the long trudge out into The Fen on your day off to show me Whimbrels).

Barrow, Alaska: Rick Lanctot, Brook Hill, and David Safine, all of the USFWS; and a big thanks to Floyd Davidson, for an adventure with the Long-tailed Jaegers.

Iowa and Missouri: Jean Braley, of Shenandoah, Iowa, and Ron Bell and the late Mike Callow, both of Squaw Creek NWR, Missouri: thanks all for your help with the Least Bitterns, years ago.

Connecticut: David Hoffman; and Dave Gumbart, of The Nature Conservancy.

Thanks to Noble Proctor, for his encouragement and interest in this project, and for a much needed nudge into the new (to me) frontier of digital photography.

For fielding my questions on shorebirds, thanks to ornithologists Joseph Jehl, of the U.S. National Museum of Natural History, and Matthew Perry, of Patuxent Wildlife Research Center.

Nobody knows the downy ducklings like Ian Gereg, and I'm enormously indebted to him for his help in identifying several orphaned loners I had photographed on prairie ponds, and in so doing saving me from some bad guesses. Thanks to ornithologist Kristof Zyskowski, at the Yale Peabody Museum of Natural History, for his help in comparing certain plumages with specimens.

Thanks to Ann Treistman, at Countryman, for her enthusiasm; and Sarah Bennett, Editorial Assistant; and for help locally with library research, Linda Alexander.

My deepest thanks to Russell Galen, one classy agent, for his persevering interest in this project.

And finally a note of gratitude to those five senior bird men, no longer here, whose encouragement has meant so much: Brooke Meanley, Powell Cottrille, Roland C. Clement, S. Dillon Ripley, and Roger Tory Peterson.

INDEX

WATER BABIES